# Organized Innovation

# ORGANIZED INNOVATION

## A Blueprint for Renewing America's Prosperity

Steven C. Currall

Ed Frauenheim

Sara Jansen Perry

*and*

Emily M. Hunter

OXFORD
UNIVERSITY PRESS

# OXFORD
UNIVERSITY PRESS

Oxford University Press is a department of the University of Oxford.
It furthers the University's objective of excellence in research, scholarship,
and education by publishing worldwide.

Oxford   New York
Auckland   Cape Town   Dar es Salaam   Hong Kong   Karachi
Kuala Lumpur   Madrid   Melbourne   Mexico City   Nairobi
New Delhi   Shanghai   Taipei   Toronto

With offices in
Argentina   Austria   Brazil   Chile   Czech Republic   France   Greece
Guatemala   Hungary   Italy   Japan   Poland   Portugal   Singapore
South Korea   Switzerland   Thailand   Turkey   Ukraine   Vietnam

Oxford is a registered trade mark of Oxford University Press
in the UK and certain other countries.

Published in the United States of America by
Oxford University Press
198 Madison Avenue, New York, NY 10016

Library of Congress Cataloging-in-Publication Data
Currall, Steven Christian.
  Organized innovation : a blueprint for renewing America's prosperity / Steven C.
Currall, Ed Frauenheim, Sara Jansen Perry, and Emily M. Hunter.
      p.   cm.
  Includes bibliographical references.
  ISBN 978–0–19–933070–6
  1. Technological innovations—Economic aspects—United States. 2. Research,
Industrial—Economic aspects—United States. 3. Economic development—United
States.  I. Title.
  HC110.T4C87 2014
  338.973—dc23
                                                    2013024406

9780199330706

# CONTENTS

# PREFACE: RESTORING OUR "VISION"

Professor Mark Humayun and his colleagues have created a small device with a big story to tell. It is an artificial retina, whose electronics sit in a canister smaller than a dime, and that literally allows the blind to see. The device reflects a new approach to innovation that can help America find its way to a more hopeful, prosperous future.

People have been dreaming about restoring sight since ancient times. The idea took hold of Humayun when his grandmother started to go blind in 1988. Humayun was in medical school preparing to be a neurosurgeon. But his grandmother's loss of vision put him on a quest to create technology that would help people see again. He switched his focus to ophthalmology, earned his MD, and imagined an implant to send digital images to the optic nerve. But when he asked biomedical engineers to help him develop such a device, he found they spoke a different language.

"I remember trying to tell them I wanted to pass a current to stimulate the retina. I wanted to excite neurons in a blind person's eyes. They looked at me and said, 'What?' I still remember their words: 'Is it faradaic? Is it capacitive? Where's the ground? Is it a dipole, coaxial, or monopolar stimulation? What's the voltage, what's the current, what's the impedance?'" Humayun says. "I'd heard the terms *voltage* and *impedance* and *current*. But all of the other things were not something you learned in medical school. I couldn't communicate what I wanted." So Humayun did something that remains rare among American researchers: he crossed over into a different discipline. He earned a doctorate in biomedical engineering at the University of North Carolina.

Now that he knew what *faradaic, capacitive,* and *coaxial* meant, Humayun began working on a system. By 1992 he and his team of fellow researchers, then at Johns Hopkins University, had a rudimentary prototype. It consisted of an electrical current generator that relayed controlled pulses to an electrode designed to rest on a person's retina. Then came the fateful first test on a human—a man who had lost his vision fifty years earlier. Humayun flipped the switch. No reaction from the patient. The researchers spent twenty minutes checking their connections. It seemed a bust. Finally, the patient piped up: "Are you guys talking about that little tiny flicker off to the side?"

Yes, they were. Humayun's team fiddled with their controls and confirmed that they were, in fact, stimulating a very primitive form of sight. Humayun recalls the moment as one of the biggest in his life, up there with the birth of his firstborn child and his wedding. "That changed the day," he says. "I knew that I had to build this device. We made a blind person see. I couldn't just stop."


## LESSONS FROM AN ENGINEERING RESEARCH CENTER

Humayun and his key collaborators, ophthalmologist Eugene de Juan, Jr. and engineering professor Jim Weiland, continued their work on the retinal prosthesis, moving to the University of Southern California (USC) in 2001. Weiland and Humayun conducted further studies to better understand the electrical and mechanical parameters needed to make the artificial retina work. Humayun and de Juan also helped form a start-up company, Second Sight, which aimed to commercialize the implant. And in 2003 Humayun and his colleagues won a National Science Foundation (NSF) grant to launch a research center to pursue retinal prostheses and other potential medical implants.

That center—the Biomimetic MicroElectronic Systems program—is part of a broader NSF initiative called the Engineering Research Center (ERC) program. The ERC program embodies government research funding, principles of planning, teamwork, and smart management and has quietly achieved remarkable success, returning to the US economy more than tenfold the $1 billion invested in it between 1985 and 2010 (Lewis, *Engineering Research Centers*).

The USC-based ERC prompted researchers to put their basic research projects on a path toward commercial prototypes. It also cultivated connections between academics and private-sector executives, as well as between researchers of different disciplines. And it provided funding for ten years—much longer than the typical academic grant.

During Humayun's leadership of the ERC, his team hit several milestones. Most visibly, the artificial retina won approval from regulators in Europe and the Food and Drug Administration (FDA) in the United States, and began changing people's lives. The BBC broadcast a segment of a once-blind grandmother playing basketball—and making shots—with her grandson. The video went viral.

Meanwhile, Humayun and fellow researchers developed a next-generation version of the artificial retina. While the commercially approved devices have as many as 60 electrodes, allowing patients to see low-resolution images, the devices in Humayun's lab have 240 and some very early prototypes have 1,000 electrodes. With digital signal processing at the camera level as well as some sophisticated software programming related to the functioning of the electrodes, these higher-electrode-count artificial retinas could enable blind patients to walk around more independently, better read large print, and recognize faces.

As Humayun and his team expand into other applications of artificial implants, the possibilities resemble science fiction—for example, improving short-term memory loss, headaches, and depression. Whatever they accomplish, the ERC program will have played a fundamental role. Humayun says the time for reflection it afforded, as well as the continuous conversations with diverse scholars, physicians, and business leaders it cultivated, gradually opened his eyes to the expansive possibilities of implants.

The story of Mark Humayun and his artificial retina has a host of hopeful lessons. Among the biggest: the United States still can achieve fundamental technology breakthroughs. We say "still" because in the past decade or so, doubts about America's innovation leadership have crept into the national consciousness. And for good reason. Although the United States remains an innovation leader, other nations—especially China—have been gaining ground as innovation has become more important to economic prosperity. America's leadership also has been questioned as the world seeks new science and engineering solutions to tough global problems such as climate change, famine, and communicable diseases. At this pivotal time of shrinking self-confidence, in other words, Humayun and his bionic eye device help restore our vision that the United States can go large when it comes to innovation.

Another lesson from the artificial retina is that universities must play a central role in American innovation. In particular, universities can help close the research and development (R&D) gap that has emerged over the past few decades. That gap is the result of US companies shifting resources away from basic research efforts to more limited, applied research and product development efforts. With the decline of Bell Labs, Xerox PARC, and other corporate research centers, US universities took on more of the basic research duties. But thanks partly to an academic culture that is often insular and discipline bound, universities and companies have often failed to work together effectively to commercialize new insights.

Humayun's team proves that, with a practical mind-set and the proper organizational structure, professors can produce powerful discoveries that turn into prototypes, life-changing products, and the beginnings of entirely new industries.

The artificial retina also exposes several myths around innovation. One myth is that breakthroughs are the work of solo geniuses. To be sure, Mark Humayun is central to the tale of the artificial retina. But so are many others, including his central collaborators, Eugene de Juan, Jr. and Jim Weiland, and a range of scholars, physicians, engineers, and business leaders. Another myth is that innovations are, more often than not, accidental in nature. While moments of serendipity punctuate the story of the artificial retina, the artificial retina is much more a saga of persistence and organization. It is a breakthrough that took twenty-five years of devotion and planning among several individuals.

A third myth discredited by the eye implant is that the free market is the only way to innovation success. Several decades ago, well-funded corporate research departments did indeed generate a steady string of inventions critical to the United States' prosperity. And the private sector continues to play an indispensable role in technology innovation—as seen by the importance of the start-up company Second Sight to the development and commercialization of the artificial retina. But amid the shift in corporate spending away from fundamental research and significant uncertainty about the prospects of an artificial retina, companies were not pursuing such a device prior to Humayun.

Despite evidence such as the retinal prosthesis, these innovation myths are alive and well. They continue to blind us to the true state of the country's innovation system. It is unorganized innovation. Indeed, it is this disorderly approach to research that is endangering our future. To replicate Humayun's success story—to the benefit of both America and the world—we have to face up to those faulty assumptions around innovation breakthroughs. We need to tell a truer story about innovation and how to achieve it.

This book synthesizes the lessons of Mark Humayun's artificial retina, the ERC program overall, and recent research on innovation. We have developed a new framework we call *Organized Innovation*. Organized Innovation is *a systematic method for leading the translation of scientific discoveries into societal benefits through commercialization*. At its core is the idea that we can, to a much greater extent than generally thought possible, organize the conditions for technology breakthroughs that lead to new products, companies, and world-leading industries. Organized Innovation consists of three pillars, or "three Cs":

Channeled Curiosity
Boundary-Breaking Collaboration
Orchestrated Commercialization

*Channeled Curiosity* refers to the marriage of curiosity-driven research and strategic planning. It harnesses "blue sky," basic science projects and steers them on a path toward tangible products. Channeled Curiosity orients researchers' inquiries toward real-world problems and proofs-of-concept with commercial potential.

*Boundary-Breaking Collaboration* refers to a radical dismantling of traditional research and academic silos to spur collective creativity and problem solving. This means connecting university, private sector, and government leaders in the pursuit of innovation. Boundary-Breaking Collaboration facilitates the interactions and exchanges that prove crucial to effective technology development.

*Orchestrated Commercialization* means coaxing the different players, including researchers, entrepreneurs, financial investors, and corporations so that they make innovations real for global use. It amplifies basic scientific discoveries to the point of proofs-of-concept and beyond. Orchestrated Commercialization coordinates efforts so early-stage technology platforms can be the basis for start-up companies or can result in products marketed by existing companies. Organized Innovation provides the foundation for world-changing innovations. Universities, government, and companies can use this framework for generating fundamentally fresh insights, developing those concepts, turning them into tangible products, and bringing those products to market to the benefit of society.

## THE ORGANIZATIONAL ARCHITECTURE OF INNOVATION

How does the Organized Innovation approach differ from other perspectives on innovation? Organized Innovation stands out by taking an *organizational* view of technology development and commercialization. In other words, our approach emphasizes how leaders in universities, businesses, and government can intentionally create and control organizational processes to optimize innovation success.

In broad terms, much past thinking on innovation focused either on creativity as a largely *individual* endeavor or on innovation as a primarily *social* process. We agree individual creativity is crucial to breakthroughs and also that innovation is social. But both perspectives are limited in their power to explain how best to cultivate technology innovation. The notion that innovation is mostly about lone geniuses is a myth; innovation typically is a result of the contributions of many individuals with complementary skills. And focusing on innovation as purely a social affair can imply that the key collaborative processes are serendipitous, difficult to direct by an organization's leaders. This leaves leaders with little practical advice other than setting up foosball tables in break rooms, dot-com style, and admonishing people to connect and be creative.

Therefore, our perspective urges leaders to go beyond simply hiring bright individuals or promoting their connectivity via social network structures. We go further by describing the optimal organizational conditions for innovation, and prescribing a set of practical recommendations to help leaders create them. The "three Cs" represent the critical conditions, and for each we offer a formula for achieving success. We see university leaders, government policymakers, and business executives as having the power to work together to dramatically affect the kind and amount of innovation produced in the United States. We are convinced that leaders can be the organizational architects of a new approach to innovation. Our Organized Innovation framework is intended to serve as a blueprint for those architects.

Organized Innovation also is intended to contribute at the level of national policy. We believe that the Organized Innovation framework can serve as the genesis of a new national innovation policy that bases research funding programs on Organized Innovation principles. In particular, we propose that federal and state funding agencies devote funds to research programs that embody Organized Innovation principles and evaluate the output of such programs based on those principles. The key advantage of the principles is that they can maximize the public's return on research and development investments.

As organizational scholars, our aim in proposing the Organized Innovation framework is to offer a new blueprint for strengthening and catalyzing the organizational dynamics of the technology commercialization processes that are upstream from, and drive, economic outcomes. Our aim is not to present detailed economic analyses; we leave those to our economist colleagues. However, we are optimistic that if embraced by universities, businesses, and government, Organized Innovation will boost America's job growth, economic health, and global competitiveness.

Organized Innovation goes against the grain of widespread doubts about the ability of universities, businesses, and government to work together to solve problems, especially amid growing public deficits. But we are convinced Americans will have the courage to see the value of investing wisely in our future by committing resources to programs that embody Organized Innovation principles. Indeed, we are convinced that Organized Innovation is the best way forward for the United States when it comes to technological and economic progress.

We four authors have come to these conclusions through both experience and years of study. Steve Currall, for example, played a pivotal role in the creation of a research center consistent with the Organized Innovation vision. While holding the William and Stephanie Sick Professorship in Entrepreneurship at Rice University, he teamed up with Nobel Laureate chemistry professor Richard Smalley and other Rice colleagues in 2000 to form a center focused on science and engineering discoveries in nanotechnology. The collaboration between Smalley-the-scientist and Currall-the-business-professor exemplified the interdisciplinary thrust of Organized Innovation. Our framework draws upon Currall's experience in the Rice center, including its success in generating spin-off firms, as well as his subsequent experience leading entrepreneurship activities at University College London and the University of California, Davis. It is also informed by Currall's nearly decade-long study of Engineering Research Centers.

The resulting book before you—*Organized Innovation: A Blueprint for Renewing America's Prosperity*—is structured in simple fashion. It has three main sections: the problem, the solution, and the prescription. Chapters 1, 2, and 3 lay out the problem in terms of the high stakes of innovation success for the United States, the challenges facing the country, and the nature of its current unorganized innovation ecosystem. The middle section of the book, chapters 4 through 7, provides the solution. This section outlines the Organized Innovation framework and details each of the three pillars with the help of empirical research findings based on qualitative and quantitative data and ERC case studies. The final section, chapters 8 and 9, is our prescription for the key players in America's innovation system—universities, government, and business—as we add to the national dialogue about global competitiveness. Centrally, we argue that the Organized Innovation framework should serve as criteria for government R&D funding decisions. Even without spending a dime more than we currently do on federal R&D, Organized Innovation will allow the United States to see its best return on investment in science and engineering research.

## WHO SHOULD READ THIS BOOK?

We have written this book with several key audiences in mind. If you serve as an academic leader, government policymaker, or technology transfer professional, the ideas in *Organized Innovation* are intended to contribute to your thinking about the future of innovation and economic development. In particular, we aim to provide new ideas that architects of innovation—such as university presidents, chancellors, provosts, vice presidents of research, and deans in the sciences, engineering, medicine, and business—can use to improve the research productivity and technology transfer of their institutions and enhance broader economic development initiatives.

The community of professionals associated with offices of technology transfer, both in universities and government research labs, will find the book a source of new ideas for how to execute their duties. For the community of research scholars who study issues of innovation and technology commercialization, our framework can be used as a theoretical paradigm for hypothesis formation and empirical examinations of the drivers of innovation outputs.

Our model of improved technology commercialization also is intended to help leaders and professionals at the many regional economic development agencies throughout the country. Spurring innovation is not only a national priority, but one that regional leaders can make a central concern. In addition, elected representatives, legislative staff members, and other government officials at the national and state level will find the book to be a valuable manual for enhancing economic competitiveness.

Our book focuses on promoting innovation anchored in university-based research centers. But leaders of corporate research and development units will recognize that Channeled Curiosity, Boundary-Breaking Collaboration, and Orchestrated Commercialization are organizational capabilities that can help speed research discoveries toward marketable products. For corporations that can execute them well, those organizational capabilities can serve as a source of sustained competitive advantage in a hypercompetitive global marketplace. The book also sheds light on the complex dynamics of university–corporate alliances and provides insights that can assist corporations in making the best use of their collaborations with both universities and government agencies.

In universities, *Organized Innovation* also will be an appealing textbook for engineering school and business school courses that are focused specifically on innovation, technology commercialization, and research policy. The book also can be valuable in courses on engineering management, technology management, engineering design, and business strategy, both at the undergraduate level and in MBA programs.

Lastly, we aimed to make the writing style of *Organized Innovation* accessible and appealing to general readers interested in business and public policy trends. Indeed, we aim to stake out new ground in the vibrant current debates about national competitiveness and business strategy, which we hope will be of interest to a broad cross section of readers.

## ORGANIZED INNOVATION AND THE NEXT BIG BREAKTHROUGHS

At the moment, America has trouble seeing the roots of its troubles. But if we can discard our blinders, there's a hopeful, clear path to a more prosperous future. It is visible not only through the artificial retina, but from the nine firms that have spun off from Mark Humayun's ERC. At the same time, researchers who have worked in that ERC—which includes partner institutions such as the University of California, Santa Cruz; Caltech; and Wake Forest University—are moving out into the worlds of academia and industry, bringing the principles of more organized, interdisciplinary research with them. These ERC veterans are planting the seeds of a new bioelectrical field, with all that it promises for human health and the country's economy. Humayun is confident the dozens of people touched by his ERC will carry on its spirit. "Each one of those people, whether in academia or companies, is now growing their own lab or starting their own efforts," he says. "Sixty people are not going to solve the unemployment problem. But each one of these can multiply by hundreds, if not thousands."

We share Humayun's optimism. If we can recognize the importance of Organized Innovation, we are confident the United States can restore its vision as a technology leader, revitalize its economy, and help to resolve pressing global problems. We are confident, in other words, that America can produce many more big breakthroughs like the small device created by Mark Humayun and his colleagues.

PART ONE
*The Problem*

# CHAPTER 1

# The Innovation Imperative

To see the importance of innovation to America and the world, take a look at David Balsley. Balsley is a fifty-two-year-old engineer at nLight, a company on the cutting edge of lasers located in the Portland, Oregon, area. Amid all the work that has shifted from the United States to lower-wage nations, Balsley and nLight are a case study in the way American workers and operations can compete internationally.

Since nLight's founding in 2000, its technology has allowed for break-throughs in areas including range finders for the military, arthroscopic surgical instruments, and tools for processing silicon chips and flat-screen displays. The company, which also has operations in Europe and Asia, has earned a spot in the Deloitte list of the five hundred fastest-growing technology companies in North America for five years running. And despite the uncertain economy, investors in 2011 poured $17.5 million into the company, bringing its funding total to some $110 million.

That money, along with revenues from customers that include the US Department of Defense, helps pay for Balsley's salary, which is more than twice the average American annual income of roughly $40,000.[1] Balsley's job enables him, his wife, Stephanie, and their two young sons to live a contemporary version of the American Dream.

The job also gives Balsley a sense of meaning at work. Lasers—harnessing the power of light to do things such as cut, weld, and transmit information—remain a largely untapped technology. It is estimated that just 50 percent of all laser applications have been realized.[2] nLight concentrates on semiconductor-based lasers, which are smaller, more efficient, and more versatile than other forms of lasers. The company also produces "fiber lasers," which use optical fibers to create systems that are small, easy to cool, and easy to manufacture.

Since arriving at nLight in 2005, Balsley has worked on semiconductor lasers for medical and industrial customers, rangefinders for the US government, and laser research funded by NASA. Recently he shifted to the fiber laser team. With a master's degree in physics from San Jose State University in Silicon Valley, he is directly engaged in the sort of work he envisioned: wrestling with the laws of nature to create ever-more-useful and powerful lasers. The prototypes he is designing today may one day power such things as tiny surgical tools that can cauterize blood vessels or cut out cancer tumors, as well as allow for new manufacturing processes that advance solar energy.

As have many Americans, Balsley has seen his workload intensify in recent years. His forty-five- to fifty-hour workweeks often include calls and e-mails in the early morning to Europe and in the late evening to China. Still, all told, nLight provides Balsley with a good job, the kind of job that America needs to be happy and prosperous.

David Balsley's tale is an upbeat one—so far. There is no guarantee it will remain sunny, however. nLight remains locked in fierce competition with its rivals, including firms in Europe and Asia. And despite the potential for nLight to bring some manufacturing back to the United States from China,[3] it is possible that as the level of laser sophistication in China rises, nLight leaders could feel compelled to shift work from Portland to Shanghai. Theoretically, such a move could cost Balsley his job.

In this way, a single laser engineer shines a light on the high stakes surrounding our nation's approach to research and development. Put simply, the United States—and, indeed, the entire world—faces an innovation imperative. Innovation is the primary economic battleground of the twenty-first century.

Let us pause to define what we mean by innovation. Innovation is the conception, development, and successful deployment—the adoption or diffusion—of novel and valuable products and processes.[4] We take issue with the use of innovation as a catchall term applied to anything at all that is novel, whether it be as simple as a new company logo, as incremental as a refinement to a business software application, or as fundamental as the world's first artificial retina. We do not mean to deny the importance of the first two examples. A new corporate logo can have powerful effects on customer psyches and the consumer "experience" that has proven to be vital to companies. And modest but much-needed improvements to products and processes also can trigger business windfalls.

But when we refer to an innovation imperative facing the United States and the world at large, we are speaking primarily about discoveries relating to products, services, and policies that can have dramatic societal and economic impact by substantially reshaping the competitive market in a single industry or launching new industries. Examples of innovation platforms on this order of magnitude include electricity, the steam engine, and the transistor, the building block of modern computing and digital communications. That is not to say that innovation has to rest on a breakthrough scientific finding, such as the discovery of DNA's double-helix structure. Indeed, as author Andrew Hargadon has shown, profoundly disruptive innovations often involve a fresh combination of existing technologies or knowledge.[5]

We agree, though, with authors such as Jon Gertner and Jerald Hage that there is a meaningful distinction between relatively minor advances and major innovation breakthroughs.[6] Smaller-scale advances, such as a new game application for Facebook, may make a splash. But they tend not to form the basis of significant new job creation and sustainable prosperity for a society. To achieve that, what is generally required is a fundamental improvement in products or processes—what we would define as a new technology "platform." Examples of new platforms include the shifts from horse and buggy to automobile, from gas-lit streets and homes to electrified cities, from analog music played on vinyl records to digital music streamed over the Internet.

Jon Gertner, the author of a history of Bell Labs, notes that we fail to distinguish between profound technological leaps and mere steps when we talk about innovation today. Mervin Kelly, the Labs' long-time leader, pursued the first kind of innovation, which Gertner wrote about in a recent *New York Times* opinion piece.

> Regrettably, we now use the term [innovation] to describe almost anything. It can describe a smartphone app or a social media tool; or it can describe the transistor or the blueprint for a cellphone system. The differences are immense. One type of innovation creates a handful of jobs and modest revenues; another, the type Mr. Kelly and his colleagues at Bell Labs repeatedly sought, creates millions of jobs and a long-lasting platform for society's wealth and well-being.[7]

For decades, America dominated when it came to this kind of disruptive innovation. But that old order is dead. Other nations—especially China—have ramped up their R&D efforts and achievements.

America's ability to get better at managing research discoveries and translating them into prototypes, commercial products, companies, and industries is going to determine, to a large degree, the country's level of economic prosperity in the future. It is not a stretch to say that America's standard of living will be determined by how well we organize innovation. And in a global context, smarter approaches to innovation will be vital as the human species tackles daunting dilemmas such as global warming, communicable diseases, and the potential for worldwide food shortages.

## INNOVATION AS THE ECONOMIC BATTLEFIELD OF THE TWENTY-FIRST CENTURY

During the past few centuries, technology innovations have dramatically improved conditions for people throughout the world. More than half of the growth in US output per hour during the first half of the twentieth century can be attributed to advancements in knowledge, particularly technology.[8]

Today, most Americans and many people across the globe live in homes with electricity, running water, sewer service, and a range of labor-saving appliances and entertainment options. We enjoy personal mobility in the form of automobiles, trains, and aircraft, as well as personal connectivity through broadband telecommunications, mobile computing, and communications devices and ever-evolving social networks such as Twitter, LinkedIn, and Facebook. Technology innovations not only enabled this level of comfort and ease, but led to jobs that allowed us to afford what we have come to define as a middle-class standard of living. In many cases, the jobs were good ones—jobs like David Balsley's that pay decently, as well as satisfy our need for creativity and meaningful collaboration.

But there is a catch to all the innovation goodness. Our economy and our standard of living are increasingly dependent on technology advances. Some of the innovations that we treasure today—advanced telecommunications and relatively inexpensive, powerful devices like iPhones—have sped the integration of a global economy. That economy, in turn, exposes increasing numbers of Americans to international competition. Beginning in the 1970s and 1980s, lower wages in developing nations began threatening blue-collar Americans' wages and jobs. Millions of US manufacturing jobs moved overseas. More recently, white-collar wages and jobs have come under fire in the United States, as companies turn to lower-cost radiologists in India, graphic artists in Korea, and call center workers in the Philippines.

US politicians have occasionally responded to the global economic pressures with protectionism—policies designed to shield US industries and workers from international competition. But mostly, America's leaders have had confidence that the country's economy would "move up the value chain." That is, they have believed US workers and companies would stay a step ahead of global rivals through advanced skills, products, and services. Through innovation, in other words, by designing things like iPads, new anti-cancer drugs, and novel, must-have services like Twitter.

The extent to which the nation relies on innovation was underscored by reports in 2005 and 2010 on American competitiveness by the National Academies, which advise the country's leaders on science, engineering, and medicine. Only 4 percent of the nation's workforce is composed of scientists and engineers, the 2010 report noted, but this group disproportionately creates jobs for the other 96 percent.[9]

All signs indicate that the economic significance of technology advances will only increase in the years ahead. A recent study commissioned by General Electric of one thousand business executives in twelve countries found that 95 percent of respondents believe innovation is the main lever for a more competitive national economy. In addition, 88 percent said innovation is the best way to create jobs in their country.[10]

The very titles of the reports from the National Academies reflect the growing importance of reaching higher levels of innovation. The first was named *Rising above the Gathering Storm: Energizing and Employing America for a Brighter Economic Future,* and called on the country's policy makers to respond to heightened global competition in the areas of science and technology.[11] The follow-up report in 2010 took on an even more urgent tone in its title: *Rising above the Gathering Storm, Revisited: Rapidly Approaching Category 5.*

Written by a blue-chip panel of leaders from industry, government, and academia that includes former Intel CEO Craig Barrett, Yale University President Richard Levin, and former Undersecretary of the Army Norman Augustine, the 2010 *Gathering Storm* committee concluded that "a primary driver of the future economy and concomitant creation of jobs will be *innovation,* largely derived from advances in science and engineering."[12]

Other leading observers have drawn the same conclusion. Among them are *New York Times* columnist Thomas Friedman and Johns Hopkins University Professor Michael Mandelbaum. In their 2011 book, *That Used to Be Us,* they identify globalization and the information technology revolution as two of the four major challenges facing the country. (The other two are the threat of fossil fuels to the planet and rising national debt and annual deficits.) Friedman and Mandelbaum see innovation as central to

US competitiveness. "For the American economy to keep growing in an information age in which innovation will have a greater economic importance than ever before, research on every front will be more vital than ever before."[13] Put simply, innovation will be the chief battlefield in the global economy of the twenty-first century.

## THAT USED TO BE US: THE AMERICAN CENTURY

For much of the twentieth century, the United States outpaced the rest of the world when it came to innovation. After winning the race to build an atomic bomb, the country continued its technology leadership in many fields. Americans soared in aviation, put the first man on the moon, discovered DNA, pushed the envelope in plastics, and produced the personal computer, the Internet, and social networking software.

Experts agree on the general formula for this success. Key ingredients included a population with many ambitious immigrants, a patent system for protecting intellectual property, a forgiving bankruptcy system, well-funded private sector research labs, and a vibrant venture capital sector. Author Jerald Hage identifies another key to US success during the last century: continual focus by private sector companies on innovative products and processes.

> Many of the more successful companies maintained product innovation over extended time periods, for example, GE, Westinghouse, DuPont, RCA, and even GM, although it is hard to believe it now. In the beginning, these companies followed a policy of product innovation and then emphasized process innovations of various kinds so as to reduce the manufacturing costs.[14]

Also important to America's innovation achievements were the historical forces of a real war (World War II) and a potential one (the Cold War) and the way American leaders coordinated the efforts of private-sector firms, university researchers, and government scientists. Friedman and Mandelbaum sum up the post–World War II approach this way:

> After the war, as scientific research became crucial for technical advance and the scale and complexity of that research could no longer be adequately sustained by private companies alone, the United States led the way. The low-hanging fruit had already been plucked by tinkerers in garages, and scientific progress now required national laboratories and partnerships between government, universities, and private companies.[15]

The results have been impressive. Automotive mass production, super-sonic aircraft, the artificial heart, the industrial robot, the laser, the transistor, and recombinant DNA methods—the foundation of the bio-technology industry—were invented on American soil. So were the oral contraception pill, the light-emitting diode, the integrated circuit, the mobile phone, GPS, and magnetic resonance imaging. From 1963 to 2012, inventors residing in the United States were granted 2.96 million patents by the US Patent and Trademark Office, outpacing the number of US patents given to inventors living in other countries by 29 percent.[16]

The United States also leads the world when it comes to the publication of research articles.[17] It is considered the best country for innovation by business executives.[18] And in a recent *Businessweek* list of the most inno-vative companies, six of the top ten were based in the United States: Apple, Google, Microsoft, IBM, Amazon, and General Electric. Japan is home to two on the list: Toyota and Sony. Korea had one, LG Electronics, and China had one, automaker BYD.[19]

The United States historically has been king of the hill in industry after industry: automotive, aerospace, defense, medical devices, pharmaceuti-cals, telecommunications, computer, and the Internet. These industries have provided millions of good jobs for US workers even as they improved the quality of life for both Americans and people throughout the globe. From the perspective of technology innovation, the twentieth century can fairly be called the American century.


## A NEW CENTURY, A NEW ERA

But it is far from clear the story will be the same in the twenty-first century. To be sure, American companies and researchers have maintained their position at the forefront of many fields and have jumped out to early leads in new frontiers such as social media, gene therapy, and big data analytics. But signs point to an erosion of America's innovative power and a surge in the capabilities of other nations. Whereas in 2000 America ranked first among the best countries for nurturing innovation, it now ranks fourth.[20] As we will show, it is not that America is not investing in innovation. It is. In terms of some metrics, the United States is investing at an increasing pace in recent years. The point, however, is that relative to the investments that many other countries are making, the United States is falling behind.

The United States has neglected key innovation ingredients even as other countries have nurtured them. Take funding of research and development. For most of the past three decades, private industry has accounted for the majority of spending on research and development in this country.[21] But as we discuss in greater detail in the next chapter, US companies have retreated from fundamental research efforts. Having shuttered or shrunk their once-elaborate research facilities, US private sector R&D activity these days tends to be applied to short-term, incremental projects.

Meanwhile, federal funding of R&D as a fraction of GDP has dropped in the past several decades—by 60 percent between 1964 and 2004.[22] If federal R&D funding had kept up with GDP growth since the early 1980s, the federal R&D budget would today surpass $200 billion. Instead it was an estimated $140.5 billion in 2012.[23]

Since 2000, leaders in Washington have increased public investments in research. For example, US federal research spending rose 5 percent from 2008 to 2012, to an estimated $63.6 billion.[24] But overall federal R&D funding was roughly flat in inflation-adjusted terms from 2004 to 2010 and dipped in 2011 and 2012.[25] At the same time, state government deficits led to massive cuts in public university budgets—weakening another key ingredient of the American innovation system.

Overall, the United States still conducts more R&D than any other nation—31 percent of the global total in 2009. But that share has declined significantly over the past decade. The figure was 38 percent in 1999.[26] The drop corresponds with an increased share of global R&D by Asian countries, whose total slice of the pie surpassed the US share in 2009 (see figure 1.1).

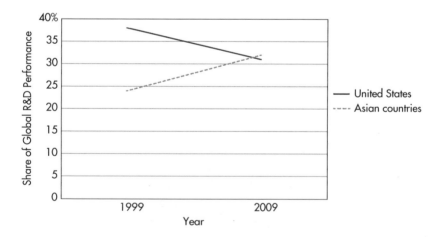

**Figure 1.1: Asia Eclipses the United States in R&D**
Credit: National Science Board, *Science and Engineering Indicators 2012* (Arlington, VA: National Science Foundation, 2012), chap. 4, http://www.nsf.gov/statistics/seind12/c4/c4h.htm.

The United States' relative slide reflects the way other nations have been making determined efforts to improve their innovation capabilities. In 2002 the European Union set a goal of devoting 3 percent of gross domestic product to R&D by 2010. Europe did not hit that goal, but it raised its R&D rate from 1.8 percent in 1998 to 2 percent in 2010. And it re-established the 3 percent goal for 2020.[27]

What's more, some key European nations are close to or are outstripping the United States when it comes to relative R&D investments. In 2008 the ratio of R&D spending to gross domestic product was 2.8 in the United States. This statistic, also called R&D intensity, was 2.7 in Germany, 2.9 in Denmark, and 3.7 in both Sweden and Finland. Japan also outdid America on this crucial foundation of innovation, allocating about 3.5 percent of GDP to research and development.[28]

Then there's China. In recent years, the country has made a conscious push to move from merely "Made in China" to "Invented in China." It seems determined to put its money, people power, and mettle behind that motto. The country's five-year plan for 2011 through 2015 calls for raising R&D spending from 1.75 percent to 2.2 percent of GDP.[29] It got off to a strong start in 2011, ramping up R&D spending by 21.9 percent to 1.83 percent of GDP—which itself grew at the rapid rate of 9.2 percent. In that one year, China constructed 130 national engineering research centers and 119 national engineering laboratories.[30]

At this point, China is producing legions of people with training in the sciences. In 2007 China became second only to the United States in the estimated number of people engaged in scientific and engineering research and development.[31] In all disciplines, the number of PhDs produced in China has jumped from about ten thousand annually in 2000 to roughly fifty thousand in 2009. By some counts, China has become the world's biggest producer of PhDs.[32]

To be sure, there are concerns about the uneven quality of Chinese PhDs—in part because programs are a relatively short three years in length. Still, China's education push comes amid doubts about America's education system. The World Economic Forum ranks the United States forty-eighth in quality of mathematics and science education.[33] Teacher quality is a chief problem. Sixty-nine percent of US public school students in fifth through eighth grades are taught math by a teacher without a degree or certificate in mathematics, and 93 percent of those students are taught the physical sciences by a teacher without a degree or certificate in the physical sciences.[34]

A growing number of thinkers point out that America's education system is not optimally preparing young people for the emerging innovation-based economy. In a 2013 column, Thomas Friedman argued that students should graduate from high school "innovation-ready" rather than "college-ready." Quoting Harvard education specialist Tony Wagner, Friedman's column pointed out that intrinsic motivation is vital to students' ability to learn continuously—yet American schools tend to quash student engagement over time. "My generation had it easy," Friedman wrote. "We got to 'find' a job. But, more than ever, our kids will have to 'invent' a job."[35]

In 2000 the number of foreign students studying the physical sciences and engineering in US graduate schools surpassed the number of US students for the first time.[36] And foreigners earning PhDs immediately face temptations to leave America's shores because of another problem regarding doctorate degrees in the United States. Doctorate holders face a shrinking number of academic jobs and an industrial sector unable to take up the slack.[37] That supply-demand problem is not present in all of America's rivals. Newly minted PhDs in India and China tend to find work, and Germany has redefined the PhD as training for high-level jobs in careers outside academia.[38]

The sobering results of the international innovation race can be seen in a variety of statistics. From 1998 to 2006, the number of research articles produced in China rose from twenty thousand to eighty-three thousand, putting the country ahead of Japan, Germany, and the United Kingdom.[39] China is now second in the world to the United States in its publication of biomedical research articles, having recently surpassed Japan, the United Kingdom, Germany, Italy, France, Canada, and Spain.[40]

The number of patent applications was flat in the United States in 2009 and rose 7.5 percent in 2010. That compares favorably to Europe. Patent applications in France, Germany, and the United Kingdom, as well as at the European Patent Office, dropped 6.5 percent in 2009 and rose 7.1 percent in 2010. Japan also performed worse than the United States, with a 10.8 percent drop in patent filings in 2009 and a 1.1 percent decline in 2010. But China topped the United States and all other nations in terms of patent filing activity: patent applications in China rose 8.5 percent in 2009 and 24.3 percent in 2010.[41]

The most recent figures from the US Patent and Trademark Office also bode poorly for the country's economic future. In 2008, for the first time, the number of foreign-origin patents exceeded the number of US-origin patents. The same thing happened in 2009, 2010, and 2011 (see figure 1.2).[42]

In 2010, for the first time since *Businessweek* began compiling its list of the most innovative companies in 2005, the majority of corporations in the Top 25 were based outside the United States.[43]

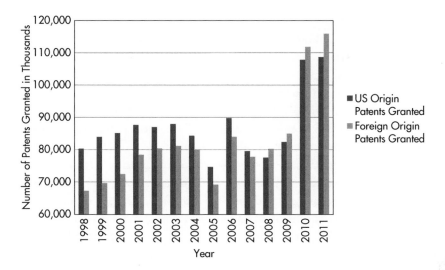

**Figure 1.2: US Patents by Country**
Credit: US Patent and Trademark Office, "Patents by Country, State, and Year—Utility Patents (December 2011)," http://www.uspto.gov/web/offices/ac/ido/oeip/taf/cst_utl.pdf.

Among China's innovation milestones: producing a supercomputer ranked in 2010 as the world's second-fastest machine; sequencing the genes of a chicken, a silkworm, and a panda; and advancing coal-gasification technology. Although people are skeptical at the sudden, somewhat amazing growth, the fact is, China is a real competitor on the innovation frontier.[44]

Global companies now are choosing to carry out innovation activities outside the United States. Among the many reasons for this shift, America's tax credit for conducting R&D on American soil is just 6 percent of the company's investment in comparison to 14 percent in China and 29 percent in Denmark.[45] Eight of the ten global companies with the largest R&D budgets have established R&D facilities in China, India, or both.[46] The offshore R&D trend includes US-based firms. GE, that prototypical American company, has now located the majority of its R&D personnel outside the United States.[47]

Hage notes that even in the high-tech sector of optoelectronics, the United States in recent years has run a trade deficit. The same is true for information and communications, as well as the life sciences.[48] As that finding suggests, the possible long-term effects of America's relative retreat on innovation are grim. Already, there are concerns that the shift of manufacturing and service work abroad has led to a "hollowing out" of the US economy—where the main work left in the country is high-paying executive jobs and low-paying service positions.

Consider electronics giant Apple. It proudly engraves on the back of iPods, iPhones, and iPads "Designed by Apple in California Assembled in China." As it stands, many more people work on the "assembled" part of the process than the "designed" part. A *New York Times* feature on work behind the iPhone estimated that Apple has some seven hundred thousand people working on its products through contractors and "almost none of them work in the United States." Meanwhile, the company employs about forty-three thousand US workers.[49]

There are signs that a "re-shoring" of manufacturing work and other jobs to the United States is under way.[50] Thanks partly to rising transportation costs and rising wages in China, companies in a range of industries are locating more work in America. Apple, for example, announced in late 2012 that some of its computers would be manufactured in the United States.

But the nascent re-shoring trend does not mean Americans can breathe easy in the global, innovation-centric economy. For example, many of Apple's US employees are highly paid professionals, including engineers and designers. But their jobs could well move overseas. As of late 2012, Apple was hiring a number of engineers in China, including a process engineer who would "lead a team of engineers . . . and others in the development and support of new module(s) (Camera, Speaker, Battery, Connectors, Trackpad, etc.) that are to be incorporated into Apple products."[51] If jobs like this one continue to be located abroad, the United States will likely suffer in tangible ways.

## INNOVATION AND GLOBAL GRAND CHALLENGES

The stakes associated with innovation go beyond Americans' standard of living and social well-being. The fate of humanity rests to a large degree on our ability to generate new solutions to tough problems. Challenges such as global warming, population growth, diminished water supplies, lethal viruses, and more sophisticated terrorists will almost certainly require technology advances in addition to political will.

In fact, the difficulties we and our planet face require new thinking about the very process of innovation, says business consultant Gary Hamel. He emphasizes that meeting our greatest challenges—problems that include climate change, global pandemics, and terrorism—demands new "innovation *systems*." These systems have to allow us to solve multidimensional and multijurisdictional problems.[52]

The thorny nature of today's problems explains what some observers see as stagnation in human innovation over the past several decades.

PayPal founder Peter Thiel recently noted in an essay that we do not travel any faster than we did in the 1960s, and we depend on the same primary sources of energy.[53] *New York Times* columnist David Brooks argues that problems often are more complicated than they appear to be at first. As examples, he points to energy alternatives, cures for cancer, and treatments for Alzheimer's. Like Hamel, Brooks suggests a fundamental shift in our conceptions around innovation. We cannot focus only on the technology if we expect to create grand innovations: we have to view the entire historical context and find new ways of seeing old problems.[54]

The Organized Innovation framework proposed in this book is a new way of seeing, a fresh perspective on innovation and commercialization, which we will explain in detail starting with chapter 4. For now, suffice it to say that the framework has the potential to accelerate and optimize our national and global progress in many arenas.

Among these is the field of lasers. Lasers under development at nLight and elsewhere could well improve everything from auto manufacturing to surgical tools to solar panels. "Lasers are going to be used across a wide range of different industries," says Scott Keeney, nLight's chief executive officer. "That's what we're excited about."

## CAN THE AMERICAN DREAM SURVIVE?

That's what David Balsley is excited about as well. But whether Balsley plays a role in any laser surgery breakthroughs or dramatic advances in solar energy will depend on nLight's continual ability to innovate. And, unless nLight innovates in the United States, the fruits of its innovations may do little to improve Americans' access to the newest surgical procedures, solar energy technologies, and flat screen displays. That is, a shift of cutting-edge laser research and development abroad could diminish the country's capacity to sustain a prosperous middle class able to afford such things as advanced medical treatments, renewable energy systems, and next-generation mobile devices.

nLight's ability to innovate domestically depends on the company's capacity to access both cutting-edge knowledge and high-quality talent. The company has been active on both these fronts. It works with local universities on theoretical research projects and sponsors student internships—many leading to full-time engineering positions.

Despite these efforts, Balsley worries that other nations are doing a better job of coordinating innovation. At the laser industry's biggest annual conference in San Francisco, he heard how German companies, in particular, have access to direct funding from their government as well as close ties to university researchers. "It often feels like American companies are at a disadvantage," he says.

Indeed, there are serious shortcomings in the US system of innovation. We address those further in the next chapter and propose solutions later in the book. It is crucial that we face up to the flaws. If we don't, David Balsley's happy tale of good work and a middle-class life—indeed the American Dream overall—could have an unhappy ending.

## NOTES

1. US Social Security Administration, "National Average Wage Index."
2. Fraunhofer-Gesellschaft, "Tailor-Made Light."
3. Sirkin, Zinser, and Hohner, *Made in America*.
4. Our definition borrows heavily from Andrew Hargadon's "Sustaining Innovation."
5. Hargadon, *How Breakthroughs Happen*.
6. See Gertner, "True Innovation," and Hage, *Restoring the Innovative Edge*.
7. Gertner, "True Innovation."
8. Solow, "Technical Change."
9. National Academies, *Gathering Storm, Revisited*, 3.
10. General Electric, *Global Innovation Barometer*.
11. National Academies, *Gathering Storm: Energizing and Employing*.
12. National Academies, *Gathering Storm, Revisited*, 2.
13. Friedman and Mandelbaum, *That Used to Be Us*, 35.
14. Hage, *Restoring the Innovative Edge*, 20.
15. Friedman and Mandelbaum, *That Used to Be Us*, 48.
16. US Patent and Trademark Office, "Patents by Country, State, and Year."
17. National Science Board, "National Science Board Releases Science and Engineering Indicators."
18. General Electric,*Global Innovation Barometer*.
19. Einhorn and Arndt, "25 Most Innovative Companies."
20. *Economist*, "Special Report," 5.
21. National Science Board, *Indicators*, appendix table 4–3.
22. Federal R&D was 1.92 percent of GDP in 1964 and 0.76 percent of GDP in 2004. See National Science Foundation, *National Patterns*, table 13.
23. Intersociety Working Group, *AAAS Report XXXVII*, highlights and chap. 2, pp. 3, 28.
24. Ibid., chap. 2, pp. 3, 25.
25. Ibid., 24.
26. National Science Board, *Indicators*, chap. 4.
27. European Commission, "R&D Expenditure."
28. Eurostat, "Gross Domestic Expenditure on R&D."
29. Casey and Koleski, *China's 12th Five-Year Plan*.
30. Xinhua News Agency, "China's R&D Spending Surges."
31. National Academies, *Gathering Storm, Revisited*, 10.

32. Cyranoski et al., "PhD Factory."
33. National Academies, *Gathering Storm, Revisited*, 6.
34. Ibid., 7–8.
35. Thomas L. Friedman, "Need a Job? Invent It," New York Times, March 30, 2013, http://www.nytimes.com/2013/03/31/opinion/sunday/friedman-need-a-job-invent-it.html, accessed July 19, 2013.
36. Ibid., 7.
37. Cyranoski et al., "PhD Factory."
38. Ibid.
39. National Academies, *Gathering Storm, Revisited*, 8.
40. Karlberg, "Biomedical Publication Trends."
41. World Intellectual Property Organization, *World Intellectual Property Indicators.*
42. US Patent and Trademark Office, "Patents by Country, State, and Year."
43. Einhorn and Arndt, "50 Most Innovative Companies."
44. Pomfret, "China Pushing the Envelope."
45. *Economist,* "Special Report."
46. National Academies, *Above the Gathering Storm, Revisited*, 7.
47. Ibid.
48. Hage, *Restoring the Innovative Edge*, 14.
49. Duhigg and Bradsher, "How the U.S. Lost Out."
50. Frauenheim, "Bringing the Jobs Back Home."
51. Apple, "Jobs at Apple."
52. Hamel, *What Matters Now,* 43.
53. Thiel, "End of the Future."
54. Brooks, "Where Are the Jobs?"

# CHAPTER 2

# Unorganized Innovation

As Phyllis Cuttino sees it, America's approach to clean energy is too messy. Serving as the director of the Pew Charitable Trusts' Clean Energy Program, Cuttino surveys the country's efforts to make advances in what's certain to be a key industry of the twenty-first century. Her observations are unsettling. A 2010 report from the Pew Environment Group found that China and Germany have taken the lead in the clean energy sector, and that the United States is falling behind on a variety of measures.[1]

For instance, by 2008 public spending in the United States on energy R&D declined to less than half what it was in the late 1970s in real purchasing power.[2] The private sector also retreated: investments in energy R&D by US companies fell by 50 percent between 1991 and 2003.[3] "The U.S. competitive position in clean energy is at risk because our policy environment is uncertain and capital is sitting on the sidelines," Cuttino wrote in a December 2011 opinion piece. "Simply put: Policy matters. Whereas China and Germany have long-term, national, clean energy policies to attract investment and spur job creation, the United States has provided limited incentives of short duration and no long-term reliability. This leaves business unable to adequately plan projects and investors searching for greener pastures."[4]

Cuttino's chief concern, in other words, is that America has been unorganized regarding energy alternatives—with debilitating results.[5] Unfortunately, her analysis of the clean energy field applies to many areas of research and development. America's method of innovation has been uncoordinated to a degree that threatens our global leadership. To be sure, the country's record of generating inventions is impressive, and it remains among the global technology leaders. But just as innovation leadership is becoming more vital to national economic success, America's position in many fields is at risk because of an unsystematic approach. Because of what we call *unorganized innovation*.

By *unorganized innovation*, we mean a system of fostering discoveries and technologies that is scattered and that has given short shrift to planning and setting priorities. It encompasses government, academia, and the private sector. It starts with a gap in the country's ability to move discoveries from the research lab to the commercial realm, and includes what amounts to national blinders about how to fix the problem.

America's lack of organization regarding innovation is rooted in the history of its corporations and universities over the past few decades, as well as misguided assumptions about innovation and economic competitiveness. As US companies shifted their energies from basic research to more limited, incremental efforts, academic scholars have taken on a larger load of fundamental research. But much scholarly work has been esoteric and limited by disciplinary boundaries. The result has been an innovation gap in America. The country has failed to bridge the gap, thanks largely to three deeply held myths about innovation that limit our ability to see a better way, as discussed in chapter 3.

## UNSYSTEMATIC RESEARCH AND DEVELOPMENT

To get a sense of how unsystematic the US approach to R&D has been in recent decades, recall some of the statistics mentioned earlier.

- Federal funding of R&D as a fraction of GDP fell by 60 percent between 1964 and 2004.[6]
- By 2008 US federal spending on energy R&D dropped to less than half of what it was in 1979 in real purchasing power.[7]

One can attribute these declines to a number of factors: America's "victory" in the Cold War and the resulting sense that the country didn't need as much defense-related R&D; budget woes related to the Iraq and Afghanistan wars and growing entitlement expenses; a recession that further sapped the country of tax revenue.

But those explanations only underscore the point that Phyllis Cuttino made about clean tech research. America has lacked a sustained public commitment to science R&D. Our annual federal budget process does have the capability to quickly increase funding in certain fields or across the board. The hike in federal spending on research in recent years is a case in point, a sign of our funding agility.[8] But overall, the process is akin to a yo-yo rather than a systematic, long-term plan for the future. Not only is America's public R&D investment inconsistent, but that funding uncertainty is also exacerbated by a patchwork quilt of subsidies and tax breaks affecting many industries. In some cases, government policy ends up buttressing old-economy industries rather than helping the country get a leg up on emerging technologies.

Government policy and investment disarray might not matter so much if the private sector were dedicated to steady investments in research and development. But, as mentioned in the previous chapter, in recent decades corporate R&D has shifted its focus from basic research that can serve as a foundation for novel technology platforms and new industries to more short-term, applied product development efforts.

In 2009 venture capitalist John Denniston took stock of the way the US private sector was investing in clean tech and was dismayed by what he saw. America's investors couldn't be counted on to lead the country into a clean tech future, concluded Denniston, a partner at the legendary Silicon Valley based venture capital firm Kleiner, Perkins, Caufield & Byers.

"In 2008 the entire venture capital industry in the US invested roughly $2.5 billion—that's with a 'b,' not a 't'—billion dollars in renewable energy research," Denniston testified to Congress. "There is no chance . . . that the venture capital industry can get us there alone."[9]

The other major player in the US science and technology landscape is academe. University scholars in science and engineering conduct a great deal of research, much of it funded by the federal government. But most academic research remains at a basic level and is not oriented toward the commercialization pipeline.

In effect, there is an innovation gap. Brad Bohlmann has a good way of communicating the problem. Bohlmann spent more than two decades as an engineer and business manager in industry before taking a position in 2010 as a leader in the Center for Compact and Efficient Fluid Power, an Engineering Research Center (ERC) based at the University of Minnesota focused on hydraulics research. Early in his career, Bohlmann worked as a project engineer on Chrysler engines and later served as engineering test lab manager at Eaton Hydraulics, a division of the industrial manufacturer Eaton, which makes products ranging from steering units to pumps to transmissions. Now Bohlmann's on the academic side, working to keep his ERC viable after its federal funding reaches its term limit, and serving as an instructor of mechanical engineering.

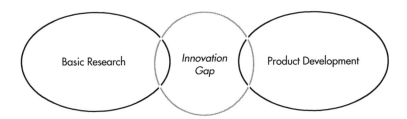

Figure 2.1: The Innovation Gap

Bohlmann summarizes the innovation gap problem with a diagram depicting two circles with a gaping hole in between (see figure 2.1). "You've got basic research over here," Bohlmann says, pointing to the far left circle. "Companies today are doing very little of that. Bell Labs are gone. This is really what academia is doing." Bohlmann now points to the far right circle. "R&D in industry really is much more "D" than "R" at this point. That's over here." Then he points to the space between those circles. "There's the 'chasm,' if you will. These two really don't touch."

The disconnect helps explain why our national innovation ecosystem has underperformed on the key issue of moving discoveries to the point of actual goods and services. The importance of addressing the shift from initial insight to commercial product was made in a 2009 report by the nonpartisan Congressional Research Service, Congress's think tank:

> The critical factor is the *commercialization* of the technology. Economic benefits accrue only when a technology or technique is brought to the marketplace where it can be sold to generate income or applied to increase productivity. Yet, while the United States has a strong basic research enterprise, foreign firms appear equally, if not more, adept at taking the results of these scientific efforts and making commercially viable products.[10]

## A BIT OF HISTORY

### The Retreat by Corporations

To understand the roots of the innovation gap, it is important to examine the history of American businesses and universities in the twentieth century. For much of the last century, companies in the United States lived by a philosophy of continual innovation in products, processes, or both. Author Jerald Hage recounts this legacy in his recent book *Restoring the*

*Innovative Edge: Driving the Evolution of Science and Technology* (2011). Hage says economic historians tend to emphasize the way US firms grew into powerhouses between the aftermath of the Civil War through the post–Second World War period by producing a standard product at a low price. Think of the way we chalk up Ford's success to the Model T, for example. But such accounts overlook the significance of original products and methods in the success:

> Frequently the company that became dominant in the United States and also worldwide did so not only with a novel product and then process innovations that achieved considerable productivity but pioneered with one or more product innovations: Such companies as Singer Sewing Machine, Diamond Match, Otis Elevators, GE, Westinghouse, DuPont, RCA, AT&T, and GM are only a few examples.[11]

Key to the innovation strategies of many of these iconic American companies was a commitment to fundamental research. Many major US businesses had well-funded laboratories that conducted basic or applied research—with an eye on the commercial implications of the explorations. The most successful of these was probably Bell Labs, the research-and-development arm of phone company AT&T.

Formed in 1925, Bell Labs generated some of the most important technologies of the twentieth century. Many of these breakthroughs continue to underpin our digital life today, including the laser, the first communications satellites, the first cellular telephone systems, and the transistor, which serves as the building block of computing devices.

But the era of big-company basic research has faded in recent decades. American firms shifted resources away from fundamental research. Bell Labs epitomized the change: in 2008, Alcatel-Lucent, which inherited Bell Labs, said it was retreating from basic physics research.[12] Statistics round out the story. Throughout most of the 1950s, US private industry contributed more than 30 percent of the nation's basic research investment. This declined to below 15 percent in the mid-1970s before recovering somewhat in the 1980s and 1990s. But industry's share of basic research spending dipped again beginning in the late 1990s. Although private-sector funding hit nearly 22 percent in 2009, the ratio was around or below 20 percent for every other year in the decade (see figure 2.2).[13]

Reasons for the move away from basic research include deregulation, as monopolies like AT&T lost their largely guaranteed revenues and profits. Heightened international competition—such as cars from Japan and computer chips from Taiwan—also pressured companies to cut costs.

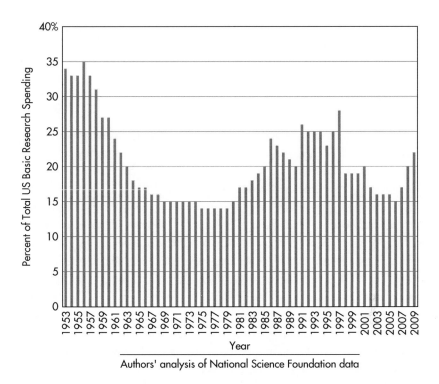

Authors' analysis of National Science Foundation data

**Figure 2.2: Industry's Share of US Basic Research Spending**
*Source*: National Science Board, *Science and Engineering Indicators 2012* (Arlington, VA: National Science Foundation, 2012), appendix, table 4–8, http://www.nsf.gov/statistics/seind12/appendix.htm#c4.

Yet another factor was the rise of a shareholder-first mindset in America in recent decades.[14] Higher, faster returns became the dominant concern among investors and executives, which tended to make long-term investments in research a lower priority. Hage sees this emphasis on profits and near-term stock returns as a key to US industry's reduced innovation prowess in the past several decades. "Rather than draw the correct lessons, namely, the need to continuously innovate new products, new processes, and new methods of distribution, the managers of industry in the post–Second World War period since the 1960s focused on the wrong measures of success—bottom lines of corporate profits and stock prices."[15] This is not to say the nation's private sector has reduced spending on R&D overall. In 2009, for example, US industry spent roughly $243 billion on internal R&D efforts—representing an inflation-adjusted increase of 7 percent from 2000.[16] But much of this activity is applied research and product development, that is, short-term, incremental projects. Although applied research can be beneficial for firms and the economy in aggregate, these constricted projects tend not to create broader technology platforms that lead to entirely new industries and their associated job gains.

### Universities into the Breach?

Industry is not the only player in the nation's innovation ecosystem, of course. Could universities, funded by federal grants, take up the slack? That was once the hope, according to Kim Stelson, director of the Center for Compact and Efficient Fluid Power at the University of Minnesota. Stelson witnessed the decline of the great corporate R&D labs firsthand. As a professor in mechanical engineering focused on novel ways to form metal, Stelson worked with corporate researchers at major industry players, including Alcoa. But when Alcoa drastically downsized basic research in the late 1980s, employees went to universities. Stelson was suddenly competing for scarce grant funds with former students who had been in industry but were forced to return to academia.

Many initially thought that this trend might mean universities could fill a void: they could do the fundamental, commercially minded research that companies were no longer pursuing. But it did not work out that way. The void, Stelson says, "persisted," and with troubling effects in his arena of mechanical engineering. "That's one of the reasons, I think, we aren't developing as much new technology as we ought to in some of these basic industries," he says. "You can't point to many revolutionary things in mechanical manufacturing—new manufacturing techniques, new approaches to vehicles or machines of any sort. I don't think so. I think basically we're in the business of just refining."

Why haven't universities filled the gap between basic research and commercial applications? The answer lies partly in the nature of academic scholarship. Our academic culture has often emphasized curiosity-driven research over practical-minded investigations. Thanks in part to a reward system that demands original discoveries, university research tends toward extreme specialization and low-impact incremental research. For instance, the journal *Science* concluded in 1990 that fewer than half of the articles published in the top science journals were cited within several years of their publication.[17]

In a 2010 commentary in the *Chronicle of Higher Education*, authors Mark Bauerlein, Mohamed Gad-el-Hak, Wayne Grody, Bill McKelvey, and Stanley W. Trimble bemoaned what they called the "Avalanche of Low-Quality Research": "While brilliant and progressive research continues apace here and there, the amount of redundant, inconsequential, and outright poor research has swelled in recent decades, filling countless pages in journals and monographs."[18] Science is valuable for the sake of new knowledge creation. And the potential usefulness of scholarship may not become clear for years or decades after its initial publication. But much of American university research is too disconnected from the needs of society. As indicated by the Congressional Research Service report mentioned previously, even when scholars make discoveries with promising technological implications, those findings often are not shepherded effectively into commercial products.

Many universities have made deep commitments to improved commercialization. Over the past few decades, universities created or expanded offices of technology transfer, and many have launched entrepreneurship centers. Federal legislators also tried to help universities to ramp up their entrepreneurial activities with the passage of the Bayh-Dole Act in 1980. The gist of the law was to allow universities to retain ownership of inventions resulting from federal funding—giving universities an incentive to sell licenses to the intellectual property and thereby commercialize it. But the law's effectiveness has been questionable.[19]

Some US universities have played vital roles in bridging the gap between basic science and commercial products. MIT and Stanford, in particular, have exemplified the way universities can channel research in practical directions. For example, Stanford has been the chief progenitor and linchpin of Silicon Valley's success.

But overall, commercialization of university-based research has not been optimal. Many people, including Stelson, place much of the blame on a social rift between scholars and businesspeople, a lack of communication. People in universities do not know where to start or how to make connections in companies, and vice versa. The Congressional Research Service report has a similar conclusion: commercialization limitations in American universities have much to do with their distance from private-sector companies over the past sixty-five years or so.

> Subsequent to World War II, the federal government supplanted industry as the primary source of funding for basic research in universities. It also became the principal determinant of the type and direction of the research performed in academia. One of the unintended consequences of this was a gulf between the academic and industrial communities. The separation and isolation of the parties involved in the innovation process is thought by many observers to be a barrier to technological progress.[20]

To be sure, there are potential conflicts of interest between universities and private-sector firms, and real risks that ties to industry can unduly influence science and even squelch important research directions. But these worries can be managed with proper guidelines and oversight. And partnerships with private sector leaders can even inspire university-based research that combines basic science with practical ends.


## Traditional Academic Training and Disciplinary Silos

Two other factors in the academic realm contribute to the country's innovation gap and exacerbate the unorganized nature of our innovation ecosystem. The first has to do with the training of science and engineering doctoral students. US universities have tended to educate future researchers for careers in academia rather than roles in the commercial sector. This emphasis is partly a function of the doctoral students' aspirations: academic research was the top career choice in a 2010 survey of 30,000 science and engineering PhD students and those at the postdoctoral level.[21] Not surprisingly, according to a 2011 *Nature* article that examined the subject, "many PhD courses train students specifically for that goal."[22]

But as the *Nature* article notes, "the proportion of people with science PhDs who get tenure-track academic positions in the sciences has been dropping steadily and industry has not fully absorbed the slack." The problem is partly a function of growing supplies of doctorates, especially in the life sciences. It also may be the case that those earning doctorates are not well suited for work on applied or basic research projects in an industrial setting. After all, doctoral students are often under pressure from their supervisors to produce research that is oriented toward academic careers, no matter how esoteric or incremental, rather than research with the potential to have commercial value.

What's more, the authors of the 2010 *Chronicle of Higher Education* commentary say the quality of science is suffering as doctoral students pursue their degrees under this model: "Aspiring researchers are turned into publish-or-perish entrepreneurs, often becoming more or less cynical about the higher ideals of the pursuit of knowledge. They fashion pathways to speedier publication, cutting corners on methodology and turning to politicking and fawning strategies for acceptance."[23] A final factor from academia figures into America's unorganized innovation system: excessive adherence to the boundaries of age-old scholarly fields. On the surface, allegiance to the limits of disciplines such as physics, mathematics, biology, and astronomy may seem to be the very essence of "organization." But when it comes to technological innovation, the most groundbreaking discoveries often occur at the intersection of areas of knowledge.[24]

It may be the case that disciplinary restrictions made sense for earlier eras of science, as researchers pursued an understanding of basic principles of physics, biology, and chemistry. To some extent, the tendency toward disciplinarity is an inescapable function of humanity's ever-expanding universe of knowledge. New discoveries and techniques in the field of biology, for example, are subdividing the discipline into multiple specialties such as computational bioinformatics, cell mechanics, and protein folding.[25] It may be necessary, therefore, for individuals to focus on particular subspecialties at least part of the time. But the problems facing the United States and the world at large are of such complexity that they typically require expertise in multiple areas. Improved solar technology energy systems, for example, may necessitate an understanding of basic physics, electrical engineering, and materials science. It is a similar situation in the biomedical field, the authors of a recent editorial in *Science* argue. "Despite the recent growth in scientific knowledge, conventional discipline-based methods have not been sufficiently effective at developing new understanding and treatments," wrote Paul Nurse, Richard Treisman, and Jim Smith of the Francis Crick Institute—a new research organization slated to open in 2015 in London.[26] There is growing appreciation of the importance of boundary-spanning collaboration in America. University faculty hiring and tenure decisions, however, are driven largely by the extent to which researchers have advanced the knowledge of their narrow field. That emphasis may have limited the ability of researchers from different disciplines—say, biologists and mechanical engineers—to join forces, and thus limited the opportunities for more complex investigations.

"Unfortunately, the dominant structures within universities for research and doctoral education make it difficult to conduct interdisciplinary research," wrote scholars Chris M. Golde and Hanna Alix Gallagher.[27] Although they drew their conclusion in 1999, academic institutions have not changed much since. Writing several years later, the authors of *The Gathering Storm* report on US competitiveness saw too little interdisciplinary research in American graduate education. They called for "education and traineeship grants to institutions focused on frontier research areas and multidisciplinary or innovation-oriented studies."[28]

Federal funding levels and procedures also contribute to the dearth of interdisciplinary investigations. In a recent editorial in *Science*, physicist James Langer made the point that physics stands on the threshold of exciting new discoveries thanks to improvements in computational and experimental capabilities. The new horizons touch on other fields such as biology and engineering—including deeper understandings of the behavior of materials in everything from jet engines to biological membranes. But these sorts of difficult problems at the intersection of traditional disciplines receive too little attention, writes Langer, who is a former vice president of the National Academy of Sciences. "Unfortunately, our ability to take advantage of these opportunities has been eroded in an environment where innovation and interdisciplinary research are systematically discouraged."[29]

The culprits, Langer says, include a too-small US research budget—such that the National Science Foundation funds only about 10 percent of the individual research proposals from scientists in his field of condensed matter and materials physics. (Recall that if federal R&D investments had kept up with GDP growth since the early 1980s, the federal R&D budget would today surpass $200 billion rather than an estimated $140.5 billion in 2012). Also to blame is a peer-review process that discourages unconventional proposals and those that bridge areas of expertise, Langer argues:

> One less-than-'excellent' review, no matter how misguided, is usually enough
> to doom a proposal. Any proposal that is truly innovative, interdisciplinary or
> otherwise unusual is almost certain to be sent to at least one reviewer who
> will be less than enthusiastic about it. Sensible investigators know not to
> submit such proposals; as a result, some of the most urgent research areas are
> disappearing.[30]

Collectively, the trends of reduced industry research investment, academically focused PhD training, and excessive disciplinarity have led to an innovation regime in the United States dominated by extremes. We are left with a paucity of truly interdisciplinary research at universities and restricted, applied research projects at companies—with what the University of Minnesota's Bohlmann called a "chasm."

This chasm may have started out small in the 1970s and 1980s, as companies slowly shifted away from research and there were high hopes universities could fill the gap. But by now, this void in science and technology research and development has widened. Although it has been obvious to many government officials, researchers, and corporate R&D leaders for a decade or more, the United States has done little about it.

Why is the country's approach to its technology future—to its very prosperity—so unorganized? After all, the stakes are high. As Phyllis Cuttino pointed out, the United States' lack of organization on clean energy puts the country at risk of losing out in this critical field. The same pattern likely holds in many other industries. The explanation for our dearth of organization has much to do with three deeply held myths in America about innovation. We examine them—and their very real consequences—in the next chapter.

## NOTES

1. Pew Charitable Trusts, *Clean Energy Race*.
2. Dooley, *U.S. Federal Investments*, 7, fig. 3.
3. Kammen and Nemet, "Reversing."
4. Cuttino, "America Needs Clean Energy Support."
5. Cuttino's concern regarding clean energy is shared by the New York Times' Thomas Friedman. In a 2013 column, Friedman made the case for a national policy requiring ever-cleaner electricity generation. He wrote: "By raising the standard a small amount every year, we'd ensure continuous innovation in clean power technologies—and jobs that are a lot better than coal mining. You can't make an appliance, power plant, factory or vehicle cleaner without making it smarter—with smarter materials, smarter software or smarter designs. Nothing would do more to ensure America's national security, stimulate more good jobs and global exports—the whole world needs these technologies—than a national clean energy standard. And, of course, the climate would hugely benefit." Friedman, "The Amazing Energy Race," *New York Times*, July 2, 2013, http://www.nytimes.com/2013/07/03/opinion/friedman-the-amazing-energy-race.html, accessed July 19, 2013.
6. Again, federal R&D was 1.92 percent of GDP in 1964 and 0.76 percent of GDP in 2004. See National Science Foundation, *National Patterns*, table 13.
7. Dooley, *U.S. Federal Investments*.
8. As mentioned in chapter 1, US federal research spending was an estimated 5 percent higher in 2012 than it was in 2008. Hourihan, "Historical Trends," 25.
9. Pentland, "Top Cleantech Countries."
10. Schacht, *Industrial Competitiveness*, 2.
11. Hage, *Restoring the Innovative Edge*, 20.
12. Slywotzky and Weber, "America's Age of Discovery."
13. National Science Board, *Indicators*, appendix tables 4–8.
14. *Economist*, "Shareholders v. Stakeholders."
15. Hage, *Restoring the Innovative Edge*, 20.
16. National Science Board, *Indicators*, appendix tables 4–7.
17. Hamilton, "Publishing by—and for?—the Numbers."
18. Bauerlein et al., "Stop the Avalanche."
19. Mowery et al., "Growth of Patenting and Licensing."
20. Schacht, *Industrial Competitiveness,* 7.
21. Cyranoski et al., "PhD Factory."
22. Ibid.
23. Bauerlein et al., "Stop the Avalanche."
24. Hunter, Perry, and Currall, "Multi-Disciplinary Science and Engineering Research Centers."
25. Benjamin F. Jones, associate professor, Kellogg School of Management, Northwestern University, e-mail message to co-author Ed Frauenheim, August 2, 2012.
26. Paul Nurse, Richard Treisman and Jim Smith, "Building Better Institutions," *Science*, July 5, 2013, Vol. 341, p. 10.
27. Golde and Gallagher, "Conducting Interdisciplinary Research," 281.
28. National Academies, *Above the Gathering Storm: Energizing*, 346.
29. Langer, "Enabling Scientific Innovation."
30. Ibid.

CHAPTER 3

# The Myths behind Unorganized Innovation

Reports from the Congressional Research Service are not usually gripping reads. Created by what is considered the think tank of the US Congress, the reports are usually written in a dry fashion, thick with policy analysis. But they can contain pearls of wisdom. One of these comes in the recent study titled *Industrial Competitiveness and Technological Advancement: Debate over Government Policy*. Author Wendy Schacht wrote: "Technology demonstration and commercialization have traditionally been considered private sector functions in the United States. While over the years there have been various programs and policies to facilitate such activities (such as tax credits, technology transfer to industry, and patents), the approach has been ad hoc and uncoordinated."[1] In this short passage, Schacht gets at the heart of America's unorganized innovation ecosystem. In the previous chapters, we saw that just as technology innovation has become more important than ever, an innovation gap has emerged in the United States. How has the country responded? Schacht sums up what government leaders have done: taken an "ad hoc and uncoordinated" approach.

What is behind this unorganized—and suboptimal—approach? Schacht's comment puts it succinctly: Technology demonstration and commercialization—in other words, precisely the planks needed to bridge the chasm discussed in the previous chapter—have been treated as largely the province of the private sector. That belief is one component of a set of myths that have obstructed a more organized innovation ecosystem.

The belief that innovation is almost exclusively about the free market is one of three myths this chapter highlights as key misguided assumptions Americans have about innovation. The other two are that discoveries are the product of solo geniuses and that insights are largely accidental. All three beliefs amount to illusions. But, as Schacht showed in the case of our sentiments about the private sector, they have real-world consequences. Collectively, they have impeded efforts to close the innovation gap and blinded us to smarter ways of creating and commercializing technology breakthroughs. In this chapter, we spell out the myths that underpin America's unorganized innovation.

## MYTH #1: THE MARKET IS THE ONLY ANSWER

Many Americans have a deep-seated belief that innovation is all about the private sector. According to this conviction, our capitalist society owes its wealth and way of life to freewheeling entrepreneurs and unfettered captains of industry. A corollary is that attempts to orchestrate economic activity amount to stultifying central planning. In other words, the failure of communism proved definitively that government planning is counterproductive—if not an affront to human liberty—and that it must be avoided as much as possible.

To be sure, markets are an indispensable component of any innovation ecosystem. The ability of entrepreneurs and private-sector firms to explore ideas, invent products and services, and bring them to commercial markets without oppressive government regulation and strictures has been key to our national success over the past few centuries. The private sector has been a driver of innovations ranging from the Wright brothers' aircraft, the Bell Labs' transistor, and Genentech's anticancer drug Avastin.

A recent Booz and Company report on the dynamics of the San Francisco Bay Area's unique innovation ecosystem uncovered that an unusually high proportion of firms in the region are *need seekers*. These firms are especially good at identifying the need for a product or service in the marketplace and then working feverishly to address it. Need seekers tend to have the strongest alignment of innovation-focused business strategies with corporate culture. This market-attuned culture of innovation is what Booz and Company considers the "secret sauce" of the Bay Area.[2] Clearly, markets matter.

Still, America's faith in the free market—and corresponding paranoia about government involvement in the economy—tends toward fanaticism. The narrative of America as a nation of self-reliant entrepreneurs is a simplistic, romantic story we tell ourselves. And, it is one that is ultimately suboptimal.

In his 2010 book *How Markets Fail*, author John Cassidy says that over the past fifty years or so influential thinkers have peddled "utopian economics" that blindly idealize markets.[3] In a more recent *New Yorker* essay, Cassidy points out that US rhetoric about the primacy of the private sector is riddled with inconsistencies. In fact, our economic history includes frequent government intervention. Cassidy argues that fears of a rising Beijing "consensus" defined by a heavy state role in the economy ignore the way the United States relied on active government policies as it grew into an economic powerhouse in the nineteenth and twentieth centuries. And quietly, we Americans continue to accept significant government involvement in the economy. For example, a wide variety of tax breaks and subsidies supports some businesses and penalizes others.[4] Government has also intervened in the market during times of crisis: consider the way the federal government responded to the financial meltdown and great recession that began in 2008 with a bailout of the automotive industry, and a significant stimulus bill.

But America remains trapped in an ideology of laissez-faire capitalism, Cassidy says, that hamstrings our ability to respond to challenges such as a looming energy crisis. "The greatest danger that Western prosperity now faces isn't posed by any Beijing consensus; it's posed by the myth of the free market."[5] That myth leads to a lack of visionary leadership and an uncoordinated, haphazard set of policies and economic interventions. Other nations, though, have taken a much more systematic approach to economic development in general and technological innovation in particular. As mentioned earlier, both the European Union and China have publicly outlined goals for their R&D spending as a percentage of GDP. The United States has no such official policy.[6]

Statistics on patents, and anecdotes about R&D from US firms locating in China, are a sign that methodical commitments to innovation pay off. More broadly, consider the dramatic rise over the past few decades of the so-called Asian "tigers": Korea, Singapore, Malaysia, Thailand, and, more recently, Vietnam. As a number of observers have noted, these countries advanced economically not through purist laissez-faire markets, but thanks to quite active government coordination. In a number of cases, governments championed an industry or companies through tax policies or other instruments. China has come under increasing fire for gaming the international system and violating free trade rules. But there is little doubt that China's extensive planning is paying off in the form of an ever-more-sophisticated tech sector and impressive economic growth.

Sometimes it takes an outsider to dispel comforting myths or shake up conventional thinking. Andy Grove was born in a centrally planned economy—Hungary—before emigrating to the United States, becoming CEO of Intel, and helping to make the firm a global powerhouse in computer microprocessors. Grove clearly loves his adopted country. But he worries it is wearing ideological blinders. In a 2010 *Businessweek* essay, Grove argued that the decline of the Soviet Union gave the United States a false sense of security about its economic system.

> Our fundamental economic beliefs, which we have elevated from a conviction based on observation to an unquestioned truism, is that the free market is the best of all economic systems—the freer the better. Our generation has seen the decisive victory of free-market principles over planned economies. So we stick with this belief, largely oblivious to emerging evidence that while free markets beat planned economies, there may be room for a modification that is even better.[7]

We have reservations about Grove's broader call for protectionism to boost manufacturing. But we share his conviction that the United States must move past a simplistic worship of free markets and corresponding demonization of government strategic thinking, which is required for visionary leadership. The notion that the free market rules all is a myth, one that ultimately restricts the nation from a smarter, more nuanced approach to innovation and economic success.

## MYTH #2: INNOVATION COMES FROM SOLO GENIUSES

Excessive faith in laissez-faire economics may stem, in part, from another popular myth: that innovation comes from solo geniuses. Our mental picture of the genesis of world-changing technology has at its center a single, heroic inventor. This is a deeply held assumption for most Americans, one tied to the country's self-image as a nation of rugged individualists who pull themselves up by the bootstraps. It follows from this belief that efforts to organize innovation through teams of people or institutions are bound to fail. By definition, collective activity crimps the creativity of gifted individuals and results in something "designed by committee."

There is some truth to this set of assumptions. At a basic level, human beings are individuals, and innovative ideas and technologies cannot arise without them. Intelligent, hard-driving people are at the heart of invention after invention. To a large extent, we owe modern-day comforts and delights to thinkers, tinkerers, and geniuses such as Leonardo da Vinci, Thomas Edison, Madam Curie, Henry Ford, Rosalind Franklin, and Steve Jobs.

Nonetheless, American's attribution of innovation success to individual innovators is out of balance. Unlike some other cultures that view situations more holistically, Americans are prone to home in on the solo inventor while ignoring the broader setting that gave rise to the breakthrough.[8] Indeed, our legends about inventors reflect and reinforce the perspective that one genius deserves the credit for an invention. As with our devotion to free markets, focusing so fully on the solo inventor prevents us from seeing the entire truth about innovation.

Author Malcolm Gladwell is one of the keenest observers on the shortcomings of locking onto individual genius when recounting outstanding achievement. His book *Outliers: The Story of Success* has done much to skewer the myth of lone-wolf geniuses as the heart of innovation. For one thing, he makes clear that people we would define as geniuses—those with well-above-average IQ scores—have a relatively ordinary record of accomplishment. Gladwell, for example, tells the sad story of Christopher Langan. With an IQ of 195—30 percent higher than Albert Einstein—Langan earned $250,000 on a TV quiz show and has been working on an ambitious physics treatise. But overall, his record of accomplishments is surprisingly minor. He spent much of his adult life as a bar bouncer, worked on his theories from a farmhouse rather than a prestigious university, and has published very few of his ideas. The problem, Gladwell argues, is that Langan grew up in an impoverished family and never developed the social skills and connections that turn out to be vital to breakthrough accomplishment. "He'd had to make his way alone," Gladwell writes, "and no one—not rock stars, not professional athletes, not software billionaires, and not even geniuses—ever makes it alone."[9]

In fact, in field after field, Gladwell tells a hidden story of success that is crucially dependent on social setting and personal and professional networks. It's not that achievers and innovators like nuclear scientist Robert Oppenheimer and software titan Bill Gates are not smart and driven. Gladwell cites research indicating that an IQ of about 120—20 percent above the average of 100 and lower than 140, which is commonly thought to be the threshold of "genius" intelligence—seems to be a necessary level for greatness in many fields.[10] But of the relatively large cohort of people with that level of intelligence, the ones who stand out typically benefit from the social and organizational settings in which they find themselves.

Bill Gates, for example, was sharp enough to get into Harvard. But, to a large extent, his triumphs as a technology titan owe to his early and unusual access to computers—and those had everything to do with social context and connections. As Gladwell recounts, Gates benefited from advantages including a high school with a rare computing club funded by school mothers, a chance to test software for a firm whose cofounder was a parent at the school, and the offer to help set up a computer system at a power station as a high school senior. Gates jumped at these opportunities, spending more than ten thousand hours programming as a young man.[11]

Not only do technology innovators typically attain their skills through social contexts, but their achievements themselves tend to have a strong social component. Our "solo" geniuses, that is, usually have a partner or team of people working with them in important ways. One example can be found in the oil-and-gas field. George Mitchell, head of Mitchell Energy, is widely credited with a key innovation in the extraction technology known as *fracking*, which causes fractures in rock formations to improve the collection of gas. The *Economist*, for example, portrayed Mitchell as a prototypical heroic genius for his role in increasing America's shale gas supplies:

> [T]he biggest difference was down to the efforts of one man: George Mitchell, the boss of an oil-service company, who saw the potential for improving a known technology, fracking, to get at the gas. Big oil and gas companies were interested in shale gas but could not make the breakthrough in fracking to get the gas to flow. Mr. Mitchell spent ten years and $6 million to crack the problem (surely the best-spent development money in the history of gas). Everyone, he said, told him he was just wasting his time and money.[12]

But the truth about Mitchell and fracking requires a wider lens. He built on knowledge about shale gas developed by the US Department of Energy (DoE), and later worked directly with the Department of Energy and the Gas Research Institute, an R&D organization. In fact, Mitchell Energy's first horizontal well was subsidized by the federal government, according to former Mitchell Energy geologist and vice president Dan Steward. "DoE started it, and other people took the ball and ran with it," Steward told the Breakthrough Institute think tank. "You cannot diminish DoE's involvement."[13]

For a well-known example of an innovator with crucial colleagues, consider Thomas Edison. He has long been hailed as a solitary mastermind of inventions including, most famously, the lightbulb. But that legend is largely a myth, says author Andrew Hargadon: "Edison was neither that heroic, that imaginative, nor that alone."[14]

Hargadon shows that Edison's most prolific period as an inventor was the time he spent overseeing a laboratory defined by collaboration. Roughly fifteen engineers or "muckers"—including an inner circle of five—threw themselves into a wide range of experiments and product design projects at Edison's lab in Menlo Park, New Jersey. This team toiled in a room 100 feet long and 30 feet wide, with workbenches in the center and shelves of books and materials along the walls. In this environment, the muckers often worked days on end.

In the six years of its operation, from 1876 to 1881, the lab generated innovations in areas such as telephones, phonographs, and lightbulbs leading to more than four hundred patents.[15] The lab has been described as the "most concentrated outpouring of invention in history."[16] But far from being a refuge for Edison to dream up revolutionary technologies on his own, the lab was a hive of collective activity. And many breakthroughs of the lab can be attributed to insights by Edison's assistants. Edison also liked to borrow ideas from other fields. As Hargadon and others have shown, people had been working on an incandescent light for decades before Edison. His "genius" was to synthesize their work into a working prototype and product.[17]

It is telling that another prolific source of innovation gets much less attention in the popular imagination than Thomas Edison. That source is Bell Labs. As mentioned in the previous chapter, Bell Labs generated some of the most important technologies of the twentieth century. But unlike the Menlo Park lab, Bell Labs never had a single individual at the center of the operation like Thomas Edison who could become the focus of the public's attention. To be sure, some people who worked at Bell Labs are famous in the scientific community, including transistor co-inventor William Shockley and the other winners of the seven Nobel Prizes given for work done at the Labs. But the lack of a superstar individual scientist to put a face on the organization has made it a less compelling story for Americans generally.

That's a shame because the story of Bell Labs helps balance the myth of the solo genius. It is largely a tale of institutionalizing invention, creating what author Jon Gertner calls an "idea factory" in his recent book about Bell Labs. He says that Bell Labs' now vanished "production lines" show the possibility of what collaborative efforts are capable of accomplishing.[18]

A key to Bell Labs' remarkable string of breakthroughs is the exchange of ideas that occurred at its flagship facility in Murray Hill, New Jersey. Gertner notes that under leader Mervin Kelly, researchers had to work with their doors open. The hallways outside those doors were configured to stimulate conversations. Kelly helped design the Murray Hill building so that its halls were very, very long—an architecture reminiscent of Edison's lengthy, open Menlo Park lab. The purpose was to force encounters with many colleagues, problems, and ideas. "A physicist on his way to lunch in the cafeteria was like a magnet rolling past iron filings," Gertner writes.[19]

Yet another supposed "solo genius," Steve Jobs also felt strongly about fostering impromptu exchanges through building design. While head of the digital animation studio Pixar, Jobs personally oversaw the plans for a new headquarters in which he wanted to force all employees to take frequent trips to the central atrium. He went so far as to try to put the building's only bathrooms next to the atrium, though he later had to compromise with additional bathrooms.[20]

Jobs, Kelly, and Edison all were onto something in their faith in the power of collaboration. The raw numbers show that, increasingly, scientific advances are the product of multiple minds. A study of nearly twenty million peer-reviewed academic papers and 2.1 million patents over the past fifty years found that levels of teamwork have increased in more than 95 percent of scientific arenas. Professor Ben Jones of the Kellogg School of Management at Northwestern University, who conducted the research, discovered that the most frequently cited studies in a field used to be the product of a solo author, like Einstein or Darwin. But these days, scientific papers by multiple authors get more than twice as many citations as those by individuals. And this is especially true of "home-run papers"—publications that receive at least one hundred citations. These are four and a half times as likely to be written by a group of scientists.

The reason for the shift, Jones says, has to do with specialization. The accumulation of knowledge forces researchers to develop specialized expertise. It's very hard for one person to master all the knowledge it takes to create science and engineering breakthroughs, Jones argues. Collaboration is the only way to tackle many of today's challenges. Whereas a hundred years ago, the Wright brothers could build an airplane all by themselves, he says, now Boeing and its suppliers need hundreds of engineers to design and produce a new airplane. "People are becoming more specialized because they must—as scientific and technical knowledge accumulates, people must by necessity know a declining fraction of it," Jones says. "Hence teamwork is necessary to aggregate expertise."[21]

Jones's research, along with the stories of Thomas Edison, Bill Gates, and Bell Labs, all but dispels the myth of the lone genius. But it would be wrong to go to the other extreme. The all-too-common experience of unproductive, poorly run group meetings and misguided compromises within organizations reminds us that individuals are vital to innovation. Forced teamwork can kill the creative spirit. Designs by committee can be dysfunctional. That is a risk as America becomes more receptive to collaboration. After all, we are starting to recognize the broader picture around innovation. Businesses and government and universities are taking networks and teamwork more seriously in their operations. Some even have adopted it as a mantra.

But overall in America, we still are too quick to latch onto the solo genius as the real fountain of innovation. This could be heard in all the commentary wondering how the country can produce "The Next Steve Jobs"[22] in the wake of the Apple chief's death. This taste for individual heroes is so strong that savvy innovators sometimes use it to market themselves. Edison may be the most striking case. Publicly, he proclaimed to work in a virtual vacuum as he invented the future: "When I start in to experiment with anything, I do not read the books; I don't want to know what has been done." But his own notes gave a prescription for invention that acknowledged his social context: "1st, Study the present construction. 2nd, Ask for all past experiences."[23]

If we see collaboration as key to breakthroughs, the implication is for society to foster communication and opportunities for teamwork—collective efforts like those that took place at Edison's lab. If we assume innovation is fundamentally about lone geniuses, the implication is for society to stand aside and allow innovation to proceed in an unorganized way. And if the United States accentuates that course of uncoordination, we increase the chances that the twenty-first-century version of Edison and his Menlo Park lab will pop up in Beijing or Berlin rather than in Boston.


### MYTH #3: DISCOVERIES ARE ACCIDENTAL

A third myth fueling unorganized innovation in America is that many if not most of the best ideas are accidental. Closely related to the myth of the lone genius, it holds that spontaneous flashes of brilliance and chance mistakes are the primary way we make scientific and technological progress. The assumption that innovation is essentially accidental and serendipitous in nature and cannot be organized may stem in part from public incomprehension about great achievement. In any event, the result of this belief is that it makes little sense to try to organize technological breakthroughs. At most, we should invest in pure, basic science and hope for the best.

As with the other two myths, the theory of discovery-as-accident has some evidence to support it. The consequences of fundamental scientific research cannot be predicted, and findings in one era may lie dormant for decades or centuries before being put to use. What is more, many important technologies are the result of lab mistakes. But Americans go to an extreme in believing that discoveries are accidental. Our popular fascination with fortuitous failures and "a-ha!" moments hides a full appreciation of the way vital insights stem from intentional and planned effort.

For a sense of the pervasive nature of this belief, consider some proto-typical invention stories. The apple falls on Sir Isaac Newton's head, sparking his famous insight into gravity. Alexander Fleming's untidy lab leads to a contaminated germ culture and the discovery of penicillin. An accidental spill of nitroglycerin leads Alfred Nobel to figure out how to make dynamite.

The shorthand versions of the gravity and penicillin stories have elements of the truth. In each case, however, the attention to serendipity has the effect of obscuring years of determined work, and teamwork, behind the breakthrough. Newton, for example, did not appear to be hit by an apple. Rather, watching an apple fall triggered questions about matter and attraction that he spent two decades developing into a theory of gravity.[24] For his part, Fleming did indeed find penicillin in a bacteria culture contaminated by mold. But he eventually gave up research on the substance, thinking it too difficult to mass produce and unlikely to be effective as an antibiotic in the human body. Instead, the scientists Howard Florey and Ernst Boris Chain took up the project, eventually producing enough penicillin during World War II to treat wounded Allied forces on D-Day.[25]

The story of dynamite as an accidental invention, meanwhile, seems to be entirely erroneous. One version of the tale runs that Nobel dropped a vial of notoriously unstable nitroglycerin into sawdust; another has a worker spilling the liquid onto clay. In both tellings, Nobel supposedly was surprised that no blast followed, and the insight paved the way to the creation of a stable explosive. But as Stephen R. Bown relates in his book, *A Most Damnable Invention: Dynamite, Nitrates, and the Making of the Modern World*, Nobel denied the invention came about by chance—"a claim corroborated by his assistants and his own correspondence."[26]

The idea that dynamite was an accidental discovery not only may be wrong, it also tends to hide the human intention behind this critical invention. Nobel had a deep-seated, personal desire to make explosives safer. His family owned nitroglycerin factories with a history of serious accidents, including one that killed his youngest brother. Nobel spent months testing dozens of substances before settling on clay as the optimal ingredient to pair with nitroglycerin.[27]

Despite the nuanced nature of these discoveries, Americans' attention tends to be drawn to the accidental element of the gravity, penicillin, and dynamite stories. In 2010 *Newsweek* magazine published a feature on thirteen "Lucky Discoveries" that included penicillin and dynamite.[28] The piece focused on Fleming's messy lab. It repeated the story of Nobel dropping a vial of nitroglycerin, without noting Nobel's insistence that dynamite was not an accidental discovery. It also failed to mention that Nobel conducted observations on many substances to mix with nitroglycerin and that he had lost a brother in an explosion.

The sense that innovation is about accidents more than anything else is not just in the popular consciousness. The idea also can be found in the business management literature. Gary Hamel, one of the most respected gurus of the genre, likened human ingenuity to biological evolution in his 2012 book, *What Matters Now.*

> As human beings, we are the genetic elite, the sentient, contemplating, and innovating sum of countless genetic accidents and transcription errors. Thank God for screw-ups. If life had adhered to Six Sigma rules, we'd still be slime. Whatever the future holds for us bipeds, we can be sure that happy accidents will always be essential to breakthrough innovation.[29]

The close cousin of "happy accidents" is the spontaneous flash of insight. The revelation that is unexpected and unpredictable, and that usually is experienced by the "solo genius" discussed above. The tale of Isaac Newton and the apple bonking him on the head combines the concept of the mishap with the "a-ha!" moment we often associate with brilliant thinkers.

Geoff Colvin's book about world-class performance, *Talent Is Overrated*, helps explain our propensity to view breakthrough achievements as spontaneous and ineffable. We tend to hold contradictory ideas about great achievement, Colvin writes. On the one hand, we believe hard work leads to success. On the other hand, we tend to view stand-out performers as having innate, natural-born talents. When push comes to shove, we usually stick with the latter theory. Not only does it explain why standout performers are rare, it also takes the average person off the hook. "This explanation has the additional advantage of helping most of us come to somewhat melancholy terms with our own performance. A god-given gift is a one-in-a-million thing. You have it or you don't. If you don't—and of course, most of us don't—then it follows that you should just forget now about ever coming close to greatness."[30] But as Colvin, Gladwell, and others have pointed out, the innate talent theory is plain wrong. World-class achievement in field after field—including science and math—is available to most people, if they are only willing to put in years and years of what Colvin calls "deliberate practice." Deliberate practice refers not simply to repeating an activity over and over, but to a rigorous manner of preparation where the person consciously seeks to improve at every step. It turns out, then, that flashes of insight are not divine gifts, but almost the opposite. They are the product of intentional human planning. "The chief constraint is mental, regardless of the field—even in sports, where we might think the physical demands are the hardest," Colvin writes. "Across realms, the required concentration is so intense that it's exhausting."[31]

The story of Bell Labs also belies the myth of innovation-as-accident. Crucial to the success of the Labs, according to Gertner's account, was a sense of purpose. "Our job, essentially, is to devise and develop facilities which will enable two human beings anywhere in the world to talk to each other as clearly as if they were face to face and to do this economically as well as efficiently," Oliver Buckley, a one-time vice president of the Labs, told new employees.[32]

That message was effective, according to Steven Chu, who won a Nobel Prize in 1997 for his work at Bell Labs in the early 1980s and later became the US energy secretary. Chu once said that a climate of applied science like Bell Labs "doesn't destroy a kernel of genius, it focuses the mind."[33]

Bell Labs is not the only example where a clear goal and organized effort paid off in breakthroughs. Consider the Manhattan Project, which resulted in the nuclear bombs used at the end of World War II, or the Apollo effort, which succeeded in landing the first human on the moon. Even the lightbulb, that cartoon image of a sudden epiphany, was the product of years of resolute pursuit. As Hargadon noted, people had been working on incandescent bulbs for decades before Edison's version of the technology.[34]

To challenge the notion of innovation as accidental is not to minimize the importance of basic scientific research. Time and again, the fruits of open-ended, curiosity-driven inquiries have led to world-changing discoveries and products. Conversely, it also is true that restricting innovation efforts to quite narrow aims—to the very limited product development initiatives often found in private sector companies today—is likely to result in discoveries that are merely incremental. But America by and large sees invention simplistically, as the result of mistakes or divine insights. And this view tends to skew our perspective about how to foster innovation breakthroughs. From a belief that innovation is largely about luck, it follows that attempting to organize or strive after technological advances is misguided and unnecessary. But simply waiting for divine inspiration to hit and happy accidents to happen is likely to leave our nation with fewer technology breakthroughs than we want and unhappy about the results.

## DO THE MYTHS HAVE CONSEQUENCES?

By now, we hope we have established that three myths—that the market is the exclusive province of invention, that solo geniuses are the ultimate source of breakthroughs, and that innovation is fundamentally accidental—are central to American thinking about innovation. But readers may wonder exactly how these myths play out in the actual world. How important are they, truly? Aren't federal budget deficits, partisan wrangling, and bureaucracy bigger obstacles to improved innovation? We do not deny that such factors play a role. But the foundations underlying day-to-day challenges in Washington and in government throughout the country are the three myths we have detailed in this chapter. These beliefs act as blinders on our business and political leaders, as well as on the voters who elect them. Together, they inhibit us from seeing how to close the innovation gap and establish a more effective and organized innovation ecosystem.

Lest we lose sight of the tangible effects of what Wendy Schacht accurately called our "ad hoc, uncoordinated" approach to technology innovation, let's return to the case of alternative energy, and to Phyllis Cuttino, director of the Clean Energy Program at the Pew Charitable Trusts. Countries that coordinate their policies through sound planning are better off, Cuttino argues: "Our research demonstrates that where national policy is strong, investment follows. Private finance and investment seek out and thrive in environments that offer market transparency, longevity, and consistency, and dry up in places that don't. The United States lacks such a policy."[35] We agree. But we are not far from a better approach to innovation in energy and many other fields. In the next section, we spell out our solution to America's unorganized innovation ecosystem. We offer an organizational blueprint based on the idea that innovation should be more intentional, collaborative, and coordinated.

## NOTES

1. Schacht, *Industrial Competitiveness*, 2.
2. Jaruzelski, Le Merle, and Randolph, *Culture of Innovation*, 1, vi.
3. Cassidy, *How Markets Fail*.
4. Pew's Phyllis Cuttino makes this point in her commentary about clean energy policy: "Unlike a number of conventional energy supports, some of which have been in place for more than fifty years, clean energy tax measures are more modest, and they are not permanent. The energy playing field is not level, and it is not sensible to continue to subsidize technologies of the past while inhibiting our competitive position with respect to the fastest-growing global technologies and markets." Cuttino, "America Needs Clean Energy Support."
5. Cassidy, "Enter the Dragon."
6. In a 2009 speech, President Barack Obama outlined a goal of investing 3 percent of the country's gross domestic product in research and innovation. See National Academies, "In National Academy of Sciences Speech." But the president's goal has not been codified as a policy or law, according to Joanne

Padron Carney, director of the Office of Government Relations at the American Association for the Advancement of Science. For example, unlike the European Union or China, the United States does not have a formal timeline for hitting a certain level of R&D spending as a percentage of gross domestic product. "There's no deadline," Padron Carney says. Joanne Padron Carney, interview by co-author Ed Frauenheim, August 8, 2012.

7. Grove, "How America Can Create Jobs."
8. Psychologist Richard Nisbett and others have conducted experiments demonstrating that people of different cultural backgrounds see the world differently. Among the most famous of Nisbett's studies is one in which he asked Americans and Japanese to look at an animated underwater scene. The Americans focused on a big fish swimming among smaller fish. But those from Japan paid attention to the overall scene. Japanese subjects made 70 percent more statements about aspects of the background environment than Americans, and twice as many comments about the connections between animate and inanimate objects. See Goode, "How Culture Molds Habits."
9. Gladwell, *Outliers*, 115.
10. Ibid., 79.
11. Ibid., 55.
12. *Economist*, "Gas Works."
13. Breakthrough Institute, "Interview with Dan Steward."
14. Hargadon, *How Breakthroughs Happen*, 12.
15. Ibid., 3.
16. Ibid., 15.
17. Ibid., 16.
18. Gertner, *Idea Factory*, 5.
19. Gertner, "True Innovation."
20. Isaacson, *Steve Jobs*, 431.
21. Benjamin F. Jones, associate professor, Kellogg School of Management, Northwestern University, e-mail message to co-author Ed Frauenheim, August 2, 2012. The statistics on academic collaboration and statement about the Wright brothers and Boeing come in part from Jonah Lehrer's article, "Groupthink," *New Yorker*, January 30, 2012. We confirmed and corrected some of the information with Jones after revelations that Lehrer had fabricated quotes in his book about creativity, *Imagine*.
22. See, for example, Wagner, "Educating the Next Steve Jobs."
23. Hargadon, *How Breakthroughs Happen*, 17.
24. Cohen and Smith, *Cambridge Companion to Newton*.
25. American Chemical Society, "Discovery and Development of Penicillin."
26. Bown, *Most Damnable Invention*, 80.
27. Ibid., 81.
28. Ramirez, "Lucky Discoveries."
29. Hamel, *What Matters Now*, 42.
30. Colvin, *Talent Is Overrated*, 5.
31. Ibid., 8.
32. Gertner, *Idea Factory*, 44.
33. Gertner, "True Innovation."
34. Hargadon, *How Breakthroughs Happen*, 6.
35. Cuttino, "America Needs Clean Energy Support."

PART TWO

*The Solution*

# CHAPTER 4

# The Organized Innovation Framework

For a sense of the big possibilities of Organized Innovation, consider a research center focused on the smallest of discoveries and devices. From 2001 until it ended in 2012, the Center for Biological and Environmental Nanotechnology (CBEN) at Rice University developed insights and methods for the field of nanotechnology, which refers to manipulating materials and devices at the molecular level (a nanometer is one-billionth of a meter).

Funded by the National Science Foundation (NSF), CBEN was the vision of the late Rice University chemistry professor Richard Smalley, who earned a 1996 Nobel Prize for his research into a novel, spherical form of carbon he dubbed "buckyballs."[1] Smalley dreamed of a center that produced new world-class research and put the discoveries on a path toward societal benefits through commercialization. For example, through CBEN, Smalley refined techniques for the manufacture of nanotubes, super-strong varieties of carbon sought after by the aerospace and other industries. As a member of the CBEN team, bioengineering professor Jennifer West, today a professor at Duke University, created a way to turn *nanoshells*—tiny metal capsules—into a molecular weapon against cancer. West's nanoshells are designed to heat up and kill tumor cells when exposed to certain frequencies of light. Now in clinical testing, this technology could open up an entirely new front in the battle against cancer.

Not only did CBEN plant seeds with commercial possibilities in a variety of fields, it played a crucial role in making sure the much-hyped field of nanotechnology was grounded in sound, prudent science. This included calming some of the media frenzy about the prospect of "nanobots" running amok and turning everything in their path into a "grey goo"—a concept made popular by Michael Crichton's 2002 novel, *Prey*. Those concerns were much more science fiction than science. And through media interview after interview, CBEN researchers helped clarify the real risks of designing and mass-producing new molecular substances: the possibility of introducing poisons into the environment.

"We said, 'Let's not talk about nanobots. Let's talk about toxicity,'" recalls Kristen Kulinowski, CBEN's former executive director for education and public policy. CBEN researchers including Mark Wiesner, also now at Duke, investigated the potential harmfulness of novel nanomaterials as well as how to reduce those negative effects. All told, members of the center explored both the opportunities and the possible dangers of nanotechnology. In this way, CBEN had a large impact on the science of the small.[2]

What was CBEN's secret to success? Organization and planning played a key part, says Vicki Colvin, the Rice chemistry professor who co-founded the center and served as CBEN's director throughout its lifespan. CBEN outlined ambitious goals for the ten years it was slated to receive funding from NSF: for example, using basic science to move toward conducting clinical tests of medical applications and field tests related to the toxicity of nanomaterials. Setting targets such as planting two nanotechnology devices in the body by 2010—in effect, laying the groundwork for a functional nanomedicine—stirred the researchers' passions and led them to overcome their temptation to pursue smaller pet projects on their own, Colvin says. "The natural tendency of academics is to diverge. The task is to get them to converge." She adds that CBEN's plan "was just audacious enough." And hence we see lesson one of Organized Innovation, *Channeled Curiosity*, orienting curiosity-driven research toward ambitious, real-world applications.

Breaking down traditional barriers also proved to be critical to CBEN. Academic disciplines, for example, were crossed routinely as researchers with offices located in close proximity collaborated on CBEN projects. Interdisciplinarity was "absolutely central," Kulinowski says. "We couldn't have done any of this without a center. Without the ability to walk down a hall and work with an environmental engineer. The chemists working with the environmental engineers. The bioengineers working with the physicists. That kind of interdisciplinarity was a constant."

CBEN also tore down traditional boundaries between academia, industry, and other sectors. Among the center's achievements was creating the International Council on Nanotechnology (ICON) in 2004. ICON served as a forum in which all interested parties could discuss the environmental health and safety risks of nanotechnology in a neutral setting. Business leaders from industries as diverse as semiconductors and cosmetics participated alongside science watchdog groups and government regulators. These were groups that typically did not talk to each other, yet were brought together by CBEN and its audacious goals. This lets us see lesson two of Organized Innovation, *Boundary-Breaking Collaboration*, which facilitates information flow across many diverse individuals and organizations. This flow increases the chances that scientific research will ultimately make a social and economic impact.

Yet another important feature of CBEN was the approach it took for commercializing technologies developed at the center. Colvin says that nanotechnology is such an experimental field that it may be better suited to start-ups than established companies when it comes to bringing discoveries to market. To that end, Colvin and Smalley tapped management professor Steve Currall, who then headed the Rice Alliance for Technology and Entrepreneurship at Rice University. Currall and the Alliance helped shepherd a number of start-up companies that were associated with the center, including Smalley's firm, Carbon Nanotechnologies, Inc. CBEN produced several other start-ups over the years as well. Hence, we see lesson three of Organized Innovation, *Orchestrated Commercialization*, bringing together those with different skills to move the science toward societal benefit through commercialization.

CBEN's success illustrates the power and promise of principles embodied in Organized Innovation. Just as it aided progress in nanotechnology, the framework can serve as the architecture for technology breakthroughs in many other fields. The Organized Innovation framework amounts to a new blueprint for how universities, government, and business can join forces to create technological revolutions that benefit our economy and society. This chapter outlines the framework and shows how it builds on other research and theories on innovation.


## THE RESEARCH FOUNDATION OF THE ORGANIZED INNOVATION FRAMEWORK

The Organized Innovation framework is inspired by lessons from a successful federal research initiative called the Engineering Research Centers (ERC) program. The National Science Foundation launched the ERC program in 1985 with a mission to strengthen the competitiveness of US firms through improved research and education. Although the program has evolved over the years, its central tenets remain an emphasis on interdisciplinary research, close collaboration between industry and academia, and a focus on bringing university discoveries to the commercial realm.

Key aspects of ERCs include a longer-than-usual ten years of funding, creation of a cross-disciplinary team, and a dedicated industry liaison role. Lynn Preston, the long-time leader of the ERC program, developed a novel "three-plane" strategic planning framework to guide ERC leaders on how to move inventions toward proofs-of-concept—technical demonstrations providing evidence that abstract ideas can have commercial potential, as described in detail later in this chapter. In effect, the ERC Program marked an early attempt to move away from business as usual in federally funded science and engineering research at universities, where scholars rarely collaborated, industry rarely got involved, and projects rarely aimed to create solutions to real-world problems.[3] The ERC program has not received a great deal of attention over the past quarter century from the general public, in part because of its relatively small scale. Compared to a nearly $7 billion allocation for NSF in 2011 alone, ERCs received roughly $1 billion between 1985 and 2009. But the payoff on the investment in about fifty centers during that time has been impressive. A 2010 NSF-commissioned study concluded that "the total downstream market value of ERC innovations to the US economy to date is well into the tens of billions of dollars."[4] Readers interested in the history and impacts of the ERC program will find Appendix A a useful reference.

Steve Currall learned about the ERC program through his role at Rice's CBEN. CBEN was not an ERC, but it had many features in common with ERCs and was supervised by federal officials who also managed the ERC program. Based on his experience at Rice, and while on sabbatical as a visiting scholar at the University of Chicago in 2003, Currall proposed to study the ERC program under a National Science Foundation grant designed to illuminate the centers' management features. He was awarded the grant in 2004 and enlisted the efforts of management scholars Sara Jansen Perry and Emily Hunter.

The resulting research project involved in-depth interviews of ERC leaders and participants, wide-ranging survey data, and extensive archival data on ERCs. More than 135 hours were devoted to collecting qualitative data, with more than two hundred ERC leaders and participants interviewed. Approximately 2,300 research faculty, center directors, industry partnering managers, administrative staff, graduate and undergraduate students, and postdoctoral researchers were invited to participate in an online survey, of which more than 800 responded. ERCs must annually report their financial and performance information to a third party company with which NSF contracts to collect, organize, and analyze ERC data; those archival data were collected for all active ERCs.

Appendix B provides details of the data collected for the study. Academic papers written by Perry, Currall, and Stuart (2007), and Hunter, Perry, and Currall (2011) provide further information on data collection and statistical analyses that serve as the foundation for the Organized Innovation framework. In Appendix C, research questions are presented, which scholars of innovation and entrepreneurship may wish to use to empirically test the framework. Currall, Perry, and Hunter subsequently took the broader lessons of the ERCs and teamed up with business writer Ed Frauenheim to conceive the Organized Innovation framework.

## ORGANIZED INNOVATION DEFINED

*Organized Innovation is a systematic method for leading the translation of scientific discoveries into societal benefits through commercialization.* The method is systematic in that it entails a comprehensive plan for initiating, developing, and commercializing technology innovations. Organized Innovation is directed at leaders, with practical guidance for what they can do in making purposeful choices about how to supervise and manage large-scale commercialization efforts. Our framework for translating scientific discoveries into positive commercial results has three central organizational components. We refer to them as the three pillars or the three "Cs" of Organized Innovation: *Channeled Curiosity, Boundary-Breaking Collaboration*, and *Orchestrated Commercialization*.

> *Channeled Curiosity refers to orienting curiosity-driven research toward solving real-world problems for societal benefit.* Channeled Curiosity stands in contrast to the typical extremes of purely curiosity-driven university explorations and constricted private sector product development efforts. Instead, leaders can steer "blue sky" research efforts toward down-to-earth solutions by conveying to basic scientists a vision of the potential societal or commercial impact of their discoveries. Put another way, Channeled Curiosity is an intentional combination of researchers' natural inquisitiveness and practical objectives. A key implication of Channeled Curiosity is that basic science paves the way for technology platforms that serve as the springboards for multiple start-up companies or commercial products, not solitary companies or products.
>
> *Boundary-Breaking Collaboration refers to facilitating information flow and collaboration among individuals representing different disciplines*

*and perspectives to make new research discoveries more innovative.* Boundary-Breaking Collaboration not only dismantles traditional research silos that have grown around academic disciplines such as physics, chemistry, medicine, engineering, biology, and computer science, but also connects university, private sector, and government leaders in the pursuit of innovation. Leaders can overcome cultural and communication barriers that exist among disciplines and institutions by cultivating opportunities for diverse colleagues to interact and by helping to lay the groundwork for productive interaction by creating common languages that foster mutual understanding. A key implication of Boundary-Breaking Collaboration is that it fosters the identification and novel assembly of technical components for proofs-of-concept with commercial potential.

*Orchestrated Commercialization refers to intentionally coordinating complementary players—researchers, patent officers, entrepreneurs, financial investors, and corporations—to maximize the success of the technology commercialization process.* It relies on inspiring leadership that helps all parties truly collaborate in amplifying discoveries to create products that can be brought to the market. Despite fears that too much organization tends to kill the creative spirit, leaders can act as matchmakers and brokers, recruiting the right people needed for different stages of the commercialization process. A key implication of Orchestrated Commercialization is that it translates proofs-of-concept into commercial prototypes and then into societal benefits via start-ups or existing companies.

We wish to be clear that the Organized Innovation framework centers on new research that ultimately becomes technology platforms, which are broad-based discoveries that serve as a foundation for multiple products, not single products.[5] Examples of technology platforms are categories of drugs such as beta blockers used to treat hypertension or, in information technology, higher-bandwidth telecommunication standards such as 4G LTE. Another example of a technology platform in the consumer world is the iOS mobile operating system, for which thousands of new applications are being written.

Our framework does not directly address "business model" innovation. This category of invention refers to novel approaches to managing companies, such as IBM's repackaging its technology services to help cities more effectively operate public infrastructure, and Medtronic's work to screen for heart disease and finance the distribution of medical devices in India.[6]

Business model innovations can reap dramatic rewards for companies and bring about important improvements in society. And Organized Innovation efforts can dovetail with business model innovation. New technology platforms such as highly efficient integrated circuit designs or fuel-saving hybrid engine systems can give rise to or work in tandem with new ways of bringing products or services to market. But fundamentally, our framework focuses on the traditional building blocks of technological innovation: scientific, engineering, and medical discoveries that can serve as the platform for multiple products or novel services.

## THE FRAMEWORK EXPLAINED

As shown in figure 4.1, the three pillars of the Organized Innovation framework map onto particular phases in the technology commercialization pipeline and prescribe specific levels of involvement by universities, businesses, and government throughout the pipeline.

In a simplified characterization, we refer to five phases in the commercialization pipeline. The commercialization pipeline is depicted as a linear process by which a novel idea moves toward a market and its potential

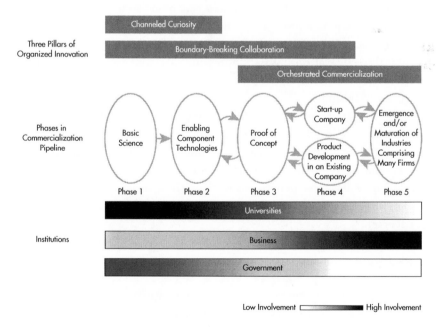

Figure 4.1: The Organized Innovation Framework

social and economic impact.[7] (In reality the process is often nonlinear, but we refer to a linear process for simplicity here and address nonlinearity and reciprocal possibilities later.)

The commercialization sequence is as follows. Typically, an idea begins within basic science at a university (Phase 1). A university researcher, who desires or is encouraged to commercialize a research discovery, then discloses it in the form of an invention disclosure. The invention disclosure is filed with the university's Technology Transfer Office (TTO), which is in charge of ensuring protection for all intellectual property arising from university employees. The TTO then determines whether to file for a patent to obtain intellectual property protection.

Beyond the initial research discovery, researchers may proceed to develop enabling component technologies (Phase 2), which serve as the pieces of the puzzle that are subsequently assembled into a "proof of concept" (Phase 3), a technical demonstration proving that an abstract scientific or engineering principle can be useful and has commercial potential.[8] It serves to demonstrate to existing companies or potential entrepreneurs that an innovation is ready to be developed into a marketable product via scale-up or manufacturing. Essentially, it provides evidence that the technology works as the inventor claims it does. This step facilitates commercialization by reducing technical risk so business leaders, entrepreneurs, and investors can focus on analyzing and mitigating other sources of risk such as market risk, scale-up risk, and risk associated with government regulation, such as approval by the Food and Drug Administration for medical products. The proof of concept idea can be extended beyond purely technical considerations by also addressing whether there is a commercial market for the technology, and exposing inventors to sources of early stage seed funding.[9]

Once the proof of concept is demonstrated, attention shifts to creation of a commercial prototype. In some fields, academic researchers also develop commercial prototypes in the lab, but in most areas, full commercial prototypes are typically produced by industry. Thus, the final product of Phase 3 may be somewhere on a spectrum from very rough proof of concept to finished prototype ready to manufacture. More often it is closer to the former.[10]

Successful prototypes can then be manufactured and launched into the market through one of two routes: licensing to a start-up company or to an existing company (Phase 4).[11] With a license, a company pays a fee or a series of royalty payments to the university in return for the right to manufacture and sell the product. Licenses generally are required to transform the university-held intellectual property into products or services; they also allow the parties to formalize a contract that addresses financial risk. Oftentimes it is preferable to launch a start-up company to manufacture and sell the product, especially if the market for the new technology is only emerging.[12] The start-up firm may be owned by the university or original researcher, or it may be a partnership among multiple individuals, potentially in conjunction with an established company.[13]

As noted, these phases are not always sequential; they may occur simultaneously or recur with feedback loops. For instance, a proof of concept in Phase 3 may reveal limitations that must be further refined in Phase 2 before a final prototype can be developed and moved to Phase 4. Success at Phase 4 may also inspire more basic science in Phase 1. General Electric, for example, has located a battery manufacturing plant in upstate New York just a few miles from the research lab where scientists invented the technology. The goal is to integrate manufacturing, design, prototyping, and production. GE views this as a simultaneous process; treating technology development as nonlinear is fundamental to their long-term competitive advantage.[14]

Phase 5 is the eventual goal of all innovations that emerge as a result of the use of Organized Innovation principles—to make a broad impact on regional, national, and global economies through job creation and economic prosperity. We recognize that small-scale, incremental innovations may be important at the level of individual inventors and companies. But the Organized Innovation framework aims to serve as a foundation for the truly groundbreaking platform innovations, those that involve larger-scale coordination and high-risk, high-reward investments. This impact might occur through development of new industries, potentially through regional clusters of start-up firms. Or it could take place through the maturation of existing industries, through the formation of an elaborated ecosystem of small, medium, and large companies as well as their suppliers, distributors, and customers. Beyond economic impact, new technologies ideally make a positive societal impact by directly improving quality of life or solving a problem facing the nation or world.

### The Scope of Each Pillar

The three pillars of Organized Innovation are specifically critical to certain phases in the commercialization pipeline. Channeled Curiosity can revolutionize the early stages of basic scientific discovery by strategically orienting curiosity-driven research toward commercializable ends and identifying the work needed to develop enabling component technologies.

Channeled Curiosity primarily operates in the transition from the basic science to enabling component technologies.

Successful advancement through much of the commercialization pipeline requires Boundary-Breaking Collaboration across academic disciplines and academic-industry boundaries. For example, the transition from Phase 3 to Phase 4 is often a crucial challenge that prevents ideas from reaching the market because established companies and entrepreneurs may be unwilling to take a gamble on an unfinished, perhaps even embryonic, proof of concept. University researchers may not always have the equipment or motivation to develop a prototype ready for a commercial user, but it is important for researchers to strive for a proof of concept that approaches prototype stage to help bridge the gap between academia and industry. As a result, Boundary-Breaking Collaboration involving input from industry partners from the beginning phases and through the entire pipeline is critical. For instance, input about needs of the public, market demands, and practical considerations may inform the proof of concept. Funding and expertise in creating commercial prototypes are often the critical missing pieces at universities, but available from industry if the right relationships are cultivated.

Orchestrated Commercialization becomes vital for bridging technologies at the proof of concept stage into concrete commercial prototypes and beyond, particularly once a technology gains momentum as a commercial prototype and is ready to be licensed and introduced to the market. Commercial execution, including cooperation between university and industry and subsequent manufacturing and scale-up of a new product, is the cornerstone of Orchestrated Commercialization.

The pillars of Organized Innovation mutually reinforce each other. Channeled Curiosity can foster Boundary-Breaking Collaboration because inventing technology with a tangible goal typically demands a diverse team. Channeled Curiosity also acts as a launching pad for Orchestrated Commercialization, as the origins of new, possibly high-impact technology platforms are explored.

Boundary-Breaking Collaboration, in turn, promotes Channeled Curiosity because multiple, diverse perspectives help generate more relevant, innovative ideas. Boundary-Breaking Collaboration also fuels Orchestrated Commercialization because the cooperation of a wide network of players inside and outside the university makes it more likely that basic science will make the leap into commercial technology platforms.

Orchestrated Commercialization may even spur new Channeled Curiosity efforts by identifying new basic science required to make commercialization possible. Without Boundary-Breaking Collaboration, it is difficult to develop truly novel research discoveries or build bridges across the academe–industry divide. In addition, Orchestrated Commercialization stimulates Boundary-Breaking Collaboration because attempts to move academic insights toward new, real-world technology platforms almost invariably require a group effort—a group that spans multiple disciplines and institutions.

Each of the three pillars of Organized Innovation is necessary but not sufficient for optimizing the commercialization of innovations. Take away Channeled Curiosity, for example, and efforts to collaborate and commercialize technology will likely lack a strong basic science foundation. That deficiency makes it less likely that the initiative will produce broad technology platforms and increases the odds of incremental, one-off products. Without Boundary-Breaking Collaboration, attempts to plan and create a new technology platform will suffer from limited perspectives and could overlook key opportunities for creative technological solutions. And in the absence of Orchestrated Commercialization, well-conceived research programs and cooperation among diverse parties will likely fall short of benefitting society because of insufficient expertise in translating prototypes into products, companies, and industries.

### Who Does What? The Roles of Universities, Businesses, and Government

With respect to institutions, Organized Innovation requires the involvement of universities, businesses, and government, as depicted in the gradient bars at the bottom of figure 4.1. Just as Channeled Curiosity, Boundary-Breaking Collaboration, and Orchestrated Commercialization serve as the crucial pillars of the framework, universities, government, and industry all are necessary institutions for its operation.

Universities, for their part, are often the sites of research discoveries that can result in new technology platforms. Collaboration across individual scholars, departments, and universities can result in breakthrough technology possibilities. Academic leaders also must work together with industry partners to design research programs that realistically can achieve the desired outcomes.[15] Universities play their most critical role in the first three phases of the commercialization pipeline—basic science through proof of concept and movement toward commercial prototypes.

Government plays the critical role of providing early seed funding of research fueling the Organized Innovation process. Government representatives also can provide crucial support to university leaders by acting as a coach or mentor to share best practices from other programs they oversee. Such guidance can come through Phase 3, but government officials perform their most important duties in the first two phases—basic science and enabling component technologies. Public officials, in concert with leading experts in relevant fields of study, should articulate mechanisms for judging the most promising projects. This typically takes the form of guidelines and reviews by government agencies such as the National Science Foundation or the National Institutes of Health. Alternatively, public officials also should draw upon the help of independent organizations such as the National Academies to create criteria for awarding funding.[16] We offer the principles of Organized Innovation for use by funding agencies to establish criteria for awarding funds. We believe that research proposals that are aligned with Organized Innovation principles should be given highest priority for funding. This is further discussed in chapter 8.

Representatives from industry are needed to help identify commercial demand for technologies on the horizon that can create new markets or solve societal problems. This may include informing the direction of basic research so that it may eventually have real-world applications. Industry partners also play a vital role in advising the efforts of university researchers in translating discoveries and early-stage inventions to marketable products. Companies help move emerging technology platforms to the market by connecting university partners with key players in the business world, such as venture capitalists, entrepreneurs, colleagues, or competitors. Businesses also can provide money, facilities, and expertise for making a proof of concept commercializable through a prototype. Ultimately, start-ups and other kinds of companies are needed to license technologies and bring new products and services to market through manufacturing, marketing, and distribution, ideally launching entire new industries. Industry is, therefore, particularly important in Phases 3 through 5 of the commercialization pipeline.

## POSSIBLE CHALLENGES TO ORGANIZED INNOVATION

Some observers will reasonably raise the possibility that academic freedom may be compromised when university professors receive industry's input into the direction of their research. Industry involvement in research raises the specter of limiting scholarly pursuits if not outright muzzling researchers. Research paid for by industry, in some cases, has resulted in such concerns.[17] Organized Innovation, though, focuses primarily on federal funding of university-based research. The main role we envision for industry is one of advice and guidance. Informing the direction of academic research and helping to move it along the commercialization pipeline does not imply that industry controls that research. Industry partners should not dictate the design of university research, prescribe the research questions, or mandate the research results. In addition, we acknowledge there is an indispensable role for curiosity-driven university research that is conducted without commercial considerations whatsoever.

Some critics may find fault with the way our approach gives influence over the use of government funds to corporations, viewing our call for industry input into university research as a form of corporate welfare that squanders public resources. But blanket opposition to collaboration with, or support of, private sector companies hinders the United States from taking smarter steps toward innovation and technology leadership— steps that are required for national prosperity in today's hypercompetitive global economy. In particular, the involvement of businesses in university-based research helps ensure that those efforts are commercial "need seeking," as mentioned in chapter 3. As demonstrated by a recent survey of San Francisco Bay Area companies designed to discover the secrets of the Bay Area's success, the best outcomes often arise from need seekers, or firms that use their deep understanding of customer needs to shape new innovations that address current or as-of-yet unarticulated needs in the market. We propose that business representatives team up with academic researchers to bring their knowledge of customers to bear on creating need-seeking products and services.[18]

Still other observers may object to our call for significant government involvement in the country's innovation ecosystem. They might consider our framework a misguided "industrial policy" that picks winners and violates free market principles. We dispute this characterization. For one thing, Organized Innovation is concerned with picking technological platforms, that is, investing in fundamental technologies with great potential to transform society and spawn many new businesses, rather than picking particular products or companies. What's more, as we discussed earlier, the US approach to innovation has deteriorated precisely because we have adopted a doctrinaire and imbalanced view of free enterprise and ignored the benefits of synergies among government, university, and industry. Together, in a coordinated way, these institutions can funnel breakthrough ideas toward society-enriching commercial platforms better than they are doing so now in our unorganized system of innovation. If any one party is missing in this formula, optimized movement through the commercialization pipeline will not occur.

The Organized Innovation framework is part of a broader push to rethink innovation. In this section, we discuss trends in innovation and show how our framework fits in with the work of other thinkers on technology and commercialization. For instance, collaboration has become a maxim in research settings and the business community. Indeed, despite the inertia that tends to keep scholars and scholarship pent up in disciplinary silos, more and more collective efforts and initiatives are underway.

Scholars Craig Boardman and Denis Gray identify a growing trend toward the creation of what they call "cooperative research centers (CRC)," which can encompass innovation centers, industry–university centers, engineering research centers, university research centers, industry consortia, and centers of excellence. Boardman and Gray define a CRC as "an organization or unit within a larger organization that performs research and also has an explicit mission (and related activities) to promote, directly or indirectly, cross-sector collaboration, knowledge and technology transfer, and ultimately innovation."[19] They note that there are more than 24,000 CRCs in the United States and Canada, and more than 13,000 CRCs in 160 other countries. Boardman and Gray see the CRC as an "increasingly important vehicle for promoting technological innovation, commercialization and, ultimately, social and economic outcomes."[20] The emergence of CRCs stems from three key developments in innovation systems worldwide: "the collectivization of research, the emergence of a cooperative paradigm for research guiding research policy in the US and abroad, and the development of open approaches to innovation by industry."[21]

The collectivization of research speaks to a point discussed in chapter 3, namely that collaborative efforts are much more likely to make a commercial impact. And the "emergence of a cooperative paradigm for research guiding research policy" parallels the thinking at NSF that gave rise to earlier initiatives such as the ERC program and the Nanoscale Science and Engineering program, which was a program funded separately from ERCs. It is also compatible with recommendations from other advisory groups that have examined innovation in various fields, for example, the Committee on a New Biology for the 21st Century.[22] That committee and others[23] concluded that the most pressing challenges faced by society can only be addressed by a coordinated scientific effort across disciplines, agencies, and organizations.[24] The development of open approaches to innovation by industry, for its part, refers to the way businesses in recent years have embraced a variety of strategies, such as crowdsourcing, that involve exposing companies to external sources of invention.

Scholar Henry Chesbrough championed the term *Open Innovation* and argues that a more open approach "offers the prospect of lower costs for innovation, faster times to market, and the chance to share risks with others."[25] Chesbrough also identifies what he calls "the growing division of innovation labor." By this he means that, increasingly, one party develops a novel idea but does not bring the idea to market itself. Rather, that party forges an alliance with or sells the idea to another party to carry the idea to market. Chesbrough refers to this as "a new organizational model of innovation, one that may offer more hopeful prospects for innovation in the future."[26] We share his optimism. The Organized Innovation framework promotes government, academic researchers, and industry partners playing different roles in the process, which dovetails with Chesbrough's observation about a division of innovation labor.

Our framework also complements Scott D. Anthony's argument that society has entered a "fourth era of innovation." He points to the importance of involving individuals working at large corporations, who are "passionate, entrepreneurial 'catalysts' who use corporations' global infrastructure, brand reputation, partner relationships, process excellence, and other capabilities to develop solutions to global challenges in ways that few others can."[27] In research centers following Organized Innovation principles, university scholars can act as partners helping corporate catalysts create change.

In general, the Organized Innovation model can give rise to "disruptive innovation," as defined by author Clayton Christensen. Christensen's theory of disruptive innovation centers on new products or services that tend to open up the bottom end of a market, such as the way personal computers toppled mainframe and minicomputer companies in the 1980s.[28] Research centers pursuing Organized Innovation can lead to technologies enabling dramatically lower price points that unseat established industries. Alternatively, Organized Innovation can stimulate entirely novel markets—such as artificial retinas or new classes of medicines.

The Organized Innovation model also builds on the work of Andrew Hargadon. We mentioned in chapter 3 that Hargadon helped dispel the myth of the individual genius inventor through his research on Thomas Edison. Research efforts pursuing Channeled Curiosity, Boundary-Breaking Collaboration, and Orchestrated Commercialization promote the "brokering" between fields described by Hargadon. We also appreciate Hargadon's cautions that collaboration efforts can reach a point of diminishing returns. "The more ties you build among different projects teams, different manufacturing plants, and different divisions, the more time it takes to maintain these ties, and the more risk there is that a common set of people, ideas and objects will come to dominate the larger community," he writes.[29] The ERC model of research thrusts (i.e., groups organized around a research theme) led by a single researcher strikes a balance between bridging different worlds and becoming a kitchen with too many chefs. We further agree with Hargadon's point that the best technology brokers do such work consciously. His call to "find and support the few people who will thrive by moving among . . . different worlds" dovetails with our belief that the leaders of ERCs and centers like them should themselves be boundary spanners.[30] We discuss such leadership questions in greater detail in chapters 5, 6, and 7.

In addition to growing attention to collaborative approaches to innovation, there has emerged in recent years an acknowledgement that focused, long-term execution matters. The growing recognition that abstract ideas or discoveries mean little if they cannot be translated into practice—and that those strategies often require patience—complements the Organized Innovation principles of Channeled Curiosity and Orchestrated Commercialization. Consider the latest book by business guru Jim Collins, *Great by Choice*. It examines companies that were exceptional in turbulent times, homing in on their ability to scale innovation, not just generate novel concepts.[31] Collins found that high-performing companies changed less in reaction to a radically changing world than other companies. "Just because your environment is rocked by dramatic change does not mean you should inflict radical change upon yourself," Collins and co-author Morten T. Hansen write. Or consider "strategic attention deficit disorder," a term coined recently by authors Teresa Amabile and Steven Kramer. "We see too many top managers start and abandon initiatives so frequently that they appear to display a kind of attention deficit disorder when it comes to strategy and tactics," Amabile and Kramer write in the January 2013 issue of the *McKinsey Quarterly*. "They don't allow sufficient time to discover whether initiatives are working."[32]

The ten-year lifespan of ERCs is a direct antidote to the short-termism that has plagued many private-sector businesses in recent decades. That extensive funding period also finds support from innovation scholar Jerald Hage, who argues that companies should select four or five high-risk, high-payoff projects and persist with them for five to ten years. "If you really want great breakthroughs, that's the only way you're going to get it," he says.[33] That longer time frame is a central requirement of the Channeled Curiosity pillar.[34]

Hage also says discussions of basic scientific research should not be divorced from manufacturing, quality, and commercialization research, which echoes the reciprocal interplay we discussed between Channeled

Curiosity and Orchestrated Commercialization. He calls for careful attention to the differences among different industries and to the way methods of innovation are themselves changing over time. Those leading innovation efforts must be nimble and aware of the big pictures in which their work exists. "Even the arenas of expertise involved in radical innovations change as new research arenas emerge and new scientific and technical training programs are created," Hage writes. "As their research arenas become distinct, managers have to be concerned about linking their research team not only with those in other research arenas but those in other sectors of the economy as well."[35] We, too, believe research center managers must be mindful of particular fields and technology maturity levels. And they must bring out the best in their researchers by exposing them to stimulating, relevant people and organizations. The process may be likened to the leader of a jazz orchestra who has a broad score to follow but will interpret it based on the particular set of musicians at his disposal, and who will seek to inspire those musicians by introducing them to other players with novel techniques and styles.

The Organized Innovation framework has a narrower focus than Hage's work, however. We concentrate on how universities in particular can be the focal points of a smarter, more coordinated approach to technology innovation. Others are making similar calls. Holden Thorp and Buck Goldstein, for example, urge universities to be "Engines of Innovation" in their 2010 book of the same title. They argue that research universities ought be more entrepreneurial and use their resources to play a lead role in solving global problems such as climate change, poverty, and childhood diseases.[36]

Recently, the National Research Council—an arm of the National Academies, which published the *Gathering Storm* warnings mentioned in chapter 1—outlined ten steps for research universities to foster the nation's prosperity and security. Among the recommendations were stable funding for university research and graduate education, a stronger business role in university research for improved technology transfer, and better prioritization of research funding.[37] We support these calls for treating universities as central to a fresh national commitment to innovation, and believe the Organized Innovation framework is the optimal approach to utilizing our universities as sources of technology invention and commercialization.

## THE FORMULA FOR THE FUTURE

The Organized Innovation framework reminds CBEN's Vicki Colvin of the philosophy she experienced while employed at one of the country's most successful research institutions, which asked researchers to explore fundamental questions *and* be mindful of commercial concerns. "That's very much Bell Labs," Colvin says. "It really is a two-way street." In many respects, CBEN showcases the wisdom and promise of the Organized Innovation framework. It not only was a trailblazer in nanotechnology research and commercialization, but it also created a methodology for examining the risks of novel technologies to address public perceptions of nanotechnology. Such perceptions are pivotal in societal adoption of new commercial applications of nanotechnology.[38] CBEN and its cousins in the ERC program have provided great inspiration for how to close the R&D gap created by decades of unorganized innovation. The answer is Organized Innovation: its three pillars provide the foundation for world-changing research and development projects. We turn in the next three chapters to explain those pillars in detail, using examples from the ERC program to illustrate the principles in practice.

**NOTES**

1. Smalley named the structures after the geodesic domes designed by inventor Buckminster Fuller.
2. CBEN was not funded through the National Science Foundation's ERC program. It was funded as an NSF Nanoscale Science and Engineering Center. CBEN, however, was overseen by the leader of the ERC program, Lynn Preston, and was required to use the three-plane strategic planning framework used by all ERCs.
3. Lynn Preston, leader of the ERC program and deputy director of the Division of Engineering Education and Centers of the Directorate for Engineering at the National Science Foundation, interview with the authors, April 4, 2013.
4. Lewis, "Engineering Research Centers."
5. Business consultant Jeffrey Phillips used the term "Organized Innovation" in a 2006 blog item about improving innovation efforts at companies. We discovered Phillips blog item only after we independently devised the phrase. Accessed June 26, 2013 from http://innovateonpurpose.blogspot.com/2006/04/organized-innovation.html
6. These examples of business model innovation are highlighted in Anthony, "New Corporate Garage."
7. See Perry, Currall, and Stuart, "Pipeline from University Laboratory," and Wood, "Process Model of Academic Entrepreneurship."
8. Myers et al., "Practitioner's View."
9. Ewing Marion Kauffman Foundation, "Proof of Concept Centers."
10. Richard Jensen and Marie Thursby demonstrate that a 1997 AUTM survey found 48 percent of inventions were at proof of concept but not prototype stage at the time of licensing, whereas 29 percent had a working prototype. See Jensen and Thursby, "Proofs and Prototypes for Sale."

11. Our framework marks a departure from the three-plane framework that NSF requires all ERCs to follow. We have amended the first three phases and added two more. We believe that Phases 4 and 5 are necessary to fully capture the process whereby basic science ultimately serves as the basis for new technology platforms.

12. Wood, "Does One Size Fit All?"

13. It is worth acknowledging that there are many paths for commercializing university research. We have discussed the common path from faculty member to start-up firm. But there are many cases of other routes, such as students creating start-up firms. Or technology may be licensed without ever involving a start-up. Moreover, there are many financing options beyond the highly visible venture capital funding model. Some early-stage companies need only small angel funding, or fund their expansion from their own revenues without any equity or debt financing. Large companies can serve as strategic investors, especially in capital-intensive industries such as energy.

14. Lowrey, "High-Tech Factories."

15. Of course, there are many obstacles to bridging these boundaries, which we discuss in detail in later chapters.

16. Physicist James Langer proposes such a system in a *Science* essay. See Langer, "Enabling Scientific Innovation."

17. Yang, "Novartis Agreement Became 'Lightning Rod.'"

18. Need seekers are distinguished from market readers, who merely look for small innovations that serve only incremental current customer needs in current industries and within current product lines. See Jaruzelski, Le Merle, and Randolph, *Culture of Innovation,* 12.

19. Boardman and Gray, "New Science and Engineering Management."

20. Ibid.

21. Ibid.

22. Committee created by the Board on Life Sciences of the National Research Council, which is the operating arm of the National Academy of Sciences, National Academy of Engineering, and the Institute of Medicine and was chartered by Congress in 1863 to advise the government on matters of science and technology. The full committee title was the "Committee on a New Biology for the 21st Century: Ensuring the United States Leads the Coming Biology Revolution." The committee's report was entitled *A New Biology for the 21st Century* and was released in August 2009. That report was sponsored by the National Science Foundation, the National Institutes of Health, and the Department of Energy. See separate endnote for full reference to report.

23. Another example is a 2013 American Academy of Arts and Sciences report, entitled "Arise 2: Unleashing America's Research and Innovation Enterprise" (Cambridge, MA). That report emphasized the importance of going beyond current interdisciplinary efforts to foster academic, government, and industry collaboration that is more comprehensive and efficient, while breaking down and redefining disciplinary boundaries. Accessed July 20, 2013 from http://www.amacad.org/multimedia/pdfs/publications/researchpapersmonographs/arise2.pdf.

24. Committee on a New Biology for the 21st Century, *New Biology.*

25. Chesbrough, *Open Business Models,* xiii.

26. Ibid., 2.

27. Anthony, "New Corporate Garage."

28. http://www.claytonchristensen.com/key-concepts/
29. Hargadon, *How Breakthroughs Happen,* 210.
30. Ibid., 211.
31. Collins and Hansen, *Great by Choice.*
32. Frauenheim, "When 'Agility' Adopts the Symptoms."
33. Frauenheim, "Delayed Innovation Gratification."
34. We acknowledge in some fields, like bioengineering, ten years may not actually be enough, but our general belief is that ten years is better than typical short-term federal grants.
35. Hage, *Restoring the Innovative Edge,* 15.
36. Thorp and Goldstein, *Engines of Innovation.*
37. Committee on Research Universities et al., *Research Universities and the Future of Americ*a.
38. Currall et al., "What Drives Public Acceptance?"

# CHAPTER 5
# Channeled Curiosity

Massachusetts Institute of Technology professor Linda Griffith knows first-hand about the power of academics channeling their curiosity toward real-world problems. Griffith herself inadvertently benefited from the work of the MIT-based Engineering Research Center she once directed. Several years after she led the Biotechnology Process Engineering Center (BPEC), Griffith was stricken with an aggressive form of breast cancer. Following her cancer diagnosis in 2010, Griffith was prescribed a drug called Neulasta, which helps patients avoid infections while their immune systems are weakened by chemotherapy. Neulasta improved on an earlier drug named Neupogen whose effects tapered off quickly. Neulasta is a biotechnology therapy—that is, a protein generated in mass quantities by turning living cells into tiny drug factories. In fact, Neulasta might be considered a second-generation biotechnology. Its longer-lasting impact reflected advanced therapy design.

Both the first and second generations of biotech protein therapy development owe much to BPEC. So does Neulasta. "The kind of protein production techniques pioneered by BPEC made it possible for me to take this drug," she says. If not a lifesaver to Griffith, Neulasta was a quality-of-life saver. Rather than have to go to a clinic every day for Neupogen shots, Griffith had an injection of Neulasta once every two weeks. That schedule allowed her to continue her research duties and to travel to New York to receive an award while keeping her immune system strong. "Neulasta made it possible for me to have the chemotherapy I had—a high-dose, high frequency chemotherapy to treat this very aggressive cancer," she says. "I never got an infection. I didn't even get mouth sores. It's a pretty miraculous drug."

A quest for medical miracles was at the heart of BPEC. For some two decades the center steered the energies and talents of researchers toward significant challenges at the intersection of biology and engineering. During its first decade from 1985 to 1995, BPEC helped usher in the era of biotechnology by developing methods to coax cells into manufacturing drugs. Renewed with a second ten-year grant, BPEC then concentrated on gene therapies and laid the foundation for advances in stem cell applications. The center played a central role in fusing the fields of biology and engineering and its legacy is visible in Griffith's current work to develop a *body on a chip*—a system of integrated artificial organs that promises to allow new insights into treating complex diseases such as diabetes. The body-on-a-chip project builds on Griffith's earlier groundbreaking work at BPEC on a *liver on a chip* device for studying liver disease.

BPEC's success at blending basic research with practical applications has much to do with the ethos of its founders, who included biologist Harvey Lodish and chemical engineer Danny Wang. Prior to the launch of BPEC, Lodish had joined with other MIT professors to advise companies in the pharmaceutical, chemical, and food industries on the impact of the emerging field of biotechnology. He and others also formed the scientific advisory board of the company that became Genzyme, one of the first successful biotech firms. About the same time, Lodish and Wang teamed up to teach the first MIT course that combined biology and engineering—a course that covered all aspects of production of recombinant proteins in cultured mammalian cells. Their efforts to bridge the divide that often separates engineering and the sciences were guided in part by a series of discussions with former students who took jobs in the drug industry. The ex-students shared the hurdles they faced as they tried to get the nascent biotechnology field off the ground. In turn, Lodish and Wang shaped their research and academic teaching to take on those obstacles. They applied for and won an ERC grant to continue their work.

To be sure, there are risks associated with directing scholarly inquiries toward commercial and social ends. The research can become cramped and incremental if tied too closely to industry's immediate needs. Conflicts of interest can arise, with the possibility that biases can taint the resulting scholarship. The passions of academics can cool if professors are funneled into projects that fail to interest them. But these challenges can be addressed. For example, Lodish and other scholars at BPEC did not abandon basic scientific inquiries. Rather, their investigations were also guided by a sense of what was important to society and industry. They paid attention to problems such as the need for better drug-production methods, methods that paved the way for drugs like the immune-system therapy that allowed

Griffith to go on with her life while fighting cancer. "The ERC fueled our research," Lodish says. "The ERC funding allowed research collaboration to expand and to relate more closely to the needs of the industry."

What Harvey Lodish, Linda Griffith, and their colleagues accomplished at BPEC captures the principle of Channeled Curiosity. Along with the other two "Cs" of the Organized Innovation framework—Boundary-Breaking Collaboration and Orchestrated Commercialization—Channeled Curiosity is a crucial ingredient in our formula for fostering technology breakthroughs. The rest of this chapter is devoted to defining Channeled Curiosity, explaining how it can be achieved, illustrating the concept with concrete examples, and addressing its potential pitfalls.

## DEFINING CHANNELED CURIOSITY

*Channeled Curiosity refers to orienting curiosity-driven research toward solving real-world problems for societal benefit.* It stands in contrast both to purely curiosity-driven academic research and to applied product development efforts at companies that lead to constrained, incremental advances. Channeled Curiosity actually ties the two extremes of R&D together. In effect, it takes what is sometimes described as "blue sky" research—investigations based on the intellectual curiosity of the researcher and without a clear goal or concrete application—and puts it on a path toward down-to-earth outcomes. Some scholars have named this type of research effort Pasteur's Quadrant, after Louis Pasteur, who exemplified it.[1] The outcomes are new technology platforms, such as novel classes of drugs, alternative vehicle engines, and digital video tagging systems.

In calling for research to be funneled toward real-world issues, we do not mean that academics should subordinate their natural inquisitiveness to the demands of industry or to commercial concerns. Rather, we are urging a kind of broad-mindedness. Think of scholars' curiosity as a river of ongoing questions. Keeping real-world impacts in mind is not to say that river should be dammed. Instead, it is routing some of that curiosity toward key issues with the potential to benefit society in important ways.

To better understand Channeled Curiosity, it is helpful to review the traditional way university science and engineering researchers pick their projects. For the most part, scholars in academic settings choose research topics based on narrow criteria. On the one hand, they are guided by what the academic literature of prior findings points to as remaining questions. On the other hand, they follow their intuition. Such curiosity-driven research may be especially prevalent after professors gain tenure and feel less pressure to gain respect among their peers. Whether the research topics are primarily driven by the scholarly community or are largely the product of individual interest, it is science for science's sake. Traditionally, the academic research enterprise is a largely self-enclosed system. Sometimes called *pure science*, it is often shielded from commercial or practical concerns, which are viewed by many academics as impurities that taint research findings.

At times, this system may give rise to groundbreaking projects with promising implications for society and the economy. But as discussed earlier, too often university scholarship is discipline-bound and deaf to the needs of the world beyond academia. Recall from chapter 2 physicist James Langer's lament about how the peer-review process stands in the way of funding for pioneering, important projects. "One less-than-'excellent' review, no matter how misguided, is usually enough to doom a proposal," he wrote. "Any proposal that is truly innovative, interdisciplinary or otherwise unusual is almost certain to be sent to at least one reviewer who will be less than enthusiastic about it."[2]

In a follow-up interview, Langer shared with us his view that basic research can be conducted with an eye toward societal needs—that in fact real-world dilemmas often require novel discoveries: "Innovative solutions to many practical problems need fundamentally new understandings of the relevant scientific principles."

## HOW TO CHANNEL CURIOSITY

We agree with Langer that basic science can be oriented toward tangible goals. But how can universities and research leaders put Channeled Curiosity into effect? Five principles are paramount:

- Lead with vision
- Pursue technology platforms
- Plan strategically
- Synthesize solutions
- Persist with the process

### Lead with Vision

First, it is important for university and research leaders to lay out a vision that defines challenging goals, such as increasing passenger vehicle fuel efficiency by 50 percent, curing a particular disease, or creating a new form of immersive, digital entertainment. By selecting big challenges, leaders will inspire scholars, administrators, and partners outside of academia, as well as attract significant public investment. Then, leaders must effectively communicate the vision to ignite the passions of researchers to work together with one another and with the outside world. Recall from chapter 4 Vicki Colvin's point that CBEN's goals such as laying the foundation for nanomedicine were "just audacious enough" to overcome the natural tendency for academics to diverge.

The vision may be specific to a particular field—such as bringing sight to the blind. Or it may be a more general mission to adopt an "entrepreneurial" mindset in academia. And there is more than one way for researchers and research centers to select the ambitious projects that support the vision. The initial prompt may be a researcher's personal preoccupation, provided it has revolutionary potential. For example, a professor's fascination with virtual reality and geographical information systems could spur thinking about how to dramatically improve applications ranging from military intelligence to education to news broadcasting. Or the seed of the project could be a major social or commercial problem, such as a need for better water conservation in urban settings that elicits questions about how to achieve that goal in fundamentally fresh ways. Whatever the specific projects, leaders should expand academe's frame of reference to include channeling their fundamental curiosities toward making a real-world impact. A compelling quest communicated well by university leaders can inspire people in multiple disciplines and in both academe and business to converge in areas they would not otherwise, all for the common goal of achieving big things.

## Pursue Technology Platforms

Related to the notion of leading with a vision for big challenges, Channeled Curiosity is about technology platforms more than it is about particular products. We define a technology platform as more basic than a technology product that may be sold to businesses or consumers. Technology platforms are foundations for multiple products and indeed entire industries. The internal combustion engine, the hypertext transfer protocol, and Apple's iOS for mobile devices are examples of platforms. Ford Mustang autos, Yahoo.com's home page, and different generations of the iPad are examples of products.

The platforms-vs.-products nature of Channeled Curiosity helps explain how the concept relates to applied research. Applied research refers to investigations undertaken for the purpose of meeting a recognized goal, such as a particular product. It often involves taking generally understood science and refining it in the service of a specific aim. As such, applied research can overlap with Channeled Curiosity. But applied research is different from Channeled Curiosity if the goal of the investigation is a product, rather than a technology platform. As they set their goals, research leaders adopting the Organized Innovation framework should take care to pursue projects likely to lead to foundational technologies and the prospect of multiple products and companies.

**Plan Strategically**

Strategic planning refers to setting long-term goals and also imagining the intermediate stages or milestones that must be reached to arrive at the intended destination. Such *planning backwards* typically requires a thorough, big-picture analysis of one or more arenas, such as the state-of-the-art in drug delivery and current limitations of the field. It also begins the synthesis process—envisioning how different technologies or discoveries could be pieced together to provide a breakthrough.

Scholars do not typically engage in strategic planning, nor is the process easy for academics accustomed to working within a single discipline, since it generally requires a broader view of multiple disciplines, of commercial markets, or of societal dilemmas. But done well, such planning has a proven track record in the business world.[3] Applied to academe, it also encourages researchers to participate in the kind of technology brokering that is crucial for technological innovation. The ERC program's three-plane framework is one tool that can help leaders of research centers effectively develop a big-picture plan. ERC leaders we interviewed repeatedly told us of the value of this particular tool, saying it "is a strategic beacon for the ERC" and it provides "a strategic timeline for where and when we are concentrating resources." Such a tool clearly adds value in an environment where planning might otherwise be difficult and not well-understood.

**Synthesize Solutions**

For Channeled Curiosity to result in breakthrough innovations, scientific researchers must do more than traditional analysis work. Analyzing a problem—pulling apart the strands of a phenomenon—will often be a part of the process. That may be necessary to arrive at crucial understandings or discoveries, such as understanding the key fuel-efficiency limitations of traditional engine designs or how mobile phone systems might shrink dramatically or how stem cells differentiate into a variety of body tissues. But after breaking down a problem, researchers must then build up a solution.

This sort of synthesis work extends beyond devising a novel object or algorithm that by itself accomplishes little. Channeled Curiosity takes aim at functional technologies—generally, taking the novel device or idea and weaving it together with other technologies. Consider the Wright brothers and their flight breakthrough. They studied aerodynamics with their wind tunnel—the analysis phase. They designed efficient propellers and wings, and more importantly, a three-axis control system for steering and maintaining equilibrium in flight. The control system is seen as their crucial advance, but they still needed to assemble a working aircraft using existing technologies such as the internal combustion engine and a version of biplane wing design. The result was their first controlled, powered flight at Kitty Hawk.[4] As the Wright brothers' experience suggests, Channeled Curiosity requires the skills of the investigator, the engineer, and the tinkerer—who ultimately pieces together a solution.

### Persist with the Process

Persistence is important because research projects in the Organized Innovation vein are likely to be fraught with challenges and require years of work before they yield desired results. The challenges may be intellectual and technical, as ambitious research quests run up against tough problems. Challenges may be organizational, as constraints and bureaucracy threaten to choke long-term Channeled Curiosity efforts. The obstacles also may be emotional, as researchers weather the criticism and even ridicule of professional peers who doubt radically alternative approaches to a problem. And those with short-attention spans will be poorly suited to pursue projects likely to last a decade or longer.

To be sure, research projects sometimes can produce technology breakthroughs in shorter order. But scholars who are familiar with spending three or four years on a dissertation study and on grant projects that generally last three years will have to demonstrate serious dedication to Channeled Curiosity efforts. Recall Jerald Hage's observation that high-risk, high-payoff projects typically take five to ten years: "If you really want great breakthroughs, that's the only way you're going to get it."

To see the principles of Channeled Curiosity in practice, let us return to the case of BPEC. The MIT center stands out among ERCs for its particularly long life. The Bioprocess Engineering Center founded by Harvey Lodish and his colleagues in 1985 did not lose its NSF funding ten years after inception. Rather, it merged into a follow-on center with the same acronym but a slightly different title. The Biotechnology Process Engineering Center received ten years of additional ERC program funding starting in 1995.

BPEC had visionary leaders who picked big challenges. In its first decade, Lodish, Wang, and others devoted themselves to the challenge of improving the development and production of therapeutic proteins. By the 1970s, scientists had realized that proteins such as human growth hormone and insulin conveyed great benefits. But there was a catch: the chief way of obtaining the prized substances involved removing the proteins from the brains of cadavers. This method was costly, limited to small volumes and existing molecules, and carried risks. Taking material from brain tissue infected some patients with prions, which cause bovine spongiform encephalopathy, or mad cow disease. As Griffith explains it, the challenge of the time was "how to make the proteins in a better, purer way. Instead of trying to extract proteins out of dead people's brains, we'd rather grow them in a lab in a very controlled way. So that you're doing it in a way that you have no possibility of having those disease-causing organisms."

The chief answer—and the foundation of modern biotechnology—was to turn mammalian cells into tiny pharmaceutical factories. BPEC researchers made numerous contributions to the emerging field of using cultured cells to produce desired proteins. For example, they figured out how to prevent in-vitro cells from sticking to bubbles and exploding upon reaching the surface. BPEC also trained a generation of scientists critical to the biotechnology industry. BPEC graduate Matthew Croughan, for example, designed a landmark biopharmaceutical facility for Genentech in 2004 involving twelve 12,000-liter fermentors. The plant in Vacaville, California, was approved by the FDA for production of a drug, even though clinical trials hadn't used that facility. Croughan and his colleagues were able to convince regulators that they had achieved enough control over the biological processes that the exact same substance created in the clinical trials would be produced in the new facility.

BPEC's second edition also set out with a vision to solve a set of weighty problems. In particular, researchers took aim at gene therapies, manipulating the DNA of patients so their own cells would produce beneficial proteins or otherwise improve health outcomes. As part of this push, BPEC researchers focused in part on stem cell therapies, which led them to explore the possibilities of tissue engineering. Center scientists also examined how to deliver therapeutic genetic material by means of synthetic vectors—essentially artificial viruses. MIT engineering professor Doug Lauffenburger, who served as BPEC director from 1998 to 2003, says the researchers wrestled with tough challenges. "These were really hard problems," he says. BPEC researchers also pursued platforms. One example is the quest for optimal synthetic DNA vectors. Those vectors were not necessarily specific to one drug product but offered the prospect of being a foundational technology for new classes of drugs.

Another platform of sorts that arose in large part from BPEC is MIT's Department of Biological Engineering. This began with the Molecular and Engineering Aspects of Biotechnology course that Lodish and Wang launched in 1986, continued with the development of a PhD program in biological engineering at MIT in 1999, and culminated with the school making Biological Engineering an undergraduate major in 2005 and an official department in 2007. Biological engineering is now one of the largest undergraduate majors at MIT, and the third-most-popular engineering concentration. The undergraduate and graduate programs continue to produce students who contribute to the evolution of biotechnology.

Today, the combination of biology and engineering seems like a no-brainer, given the profusion of biotech drugs, gene therapies, and advanced artificial joints. But back in the 1980s, the two fields were like oil and water. Engineers, for example, were wary of the life sciences, says Lauffenburger, whose training was in chemical engineering. "Biology was generally viewed to be too messy, too soft," he says.

Lodish and Wang, and later Lauffenburger and Griffith, however, developed a vision and a strategic plan to unite these once-disparate arenas. BPEC leaders also used the ERC three-plane framework to strategically plot out their research directions. For example, one way they worked to improve gene and cell therapies was through better in-vitro models. To this end, Griffith, who took over as head of BPEC in 2003, spearheaded the development of a *liver on a chip*. Scientists had struggled to understand hepatitis and other liver diseases because once liver cells were taken outside the body, they lost their ability to become infected. So Griffith and her team worked to create a kind of artificial liver.

Griffith's *liver on a chip* is also a good example of the way BPEC researchers have synthesized solutions. It required a combination of biological knowledge and mechanical cleverness. The device, smaller than a dime, took the shape of two pieces of silicon with tiny wells for rat liver cells to anchor themselves. Researchers then sealed the device in a housing and re-created the conditions of a live body, sending a fluid through it with oxygen and nutrients.[5] The *liver on a chip* not only proved helpful with research on liver disease, but served as a foundation for Griffith's more recent work on the *body on a chip* project.

Another example of a focus on synthesizing solutions relates to seminal work BPEC researchers did related to stem cells and tissue engineering. In the course of experimenting with stem cells as potential vehicles for genetic therapies, BPEC researchers developed methods of prompting the cells to differentiate into various kinds of tissues. Led in part by professor Robert Langer, those efforts translated into an experimental treatment for growing artificial skin that is now used clinically and a method for growing cartilage that was in clinical testing as of early 2013.

BPEC exemplifies persistence not only in terms of its long institutional lifespan, but through the efforts of its individual scientists. Robert Langer, for example, became one of the most prolific scholar-entrepreneurs in history only after suffering a large number of setbacks. Soon after receiving his PhD from MIT in 1974, he asked medical schools if he could apply his chemical engineering background to medical problems. More than a dozen rejected him before Harvard Medical School professor Dr. Judah Folkman gave him an opportunity. He also struggled with funding requests early in his career. Even after publishing a paper in *Science* about how the large molecules in cartilage could offer a way to block the growth of new blood vessels in cancer tumors, his first nine grant proposals were rejected.

Having persevered with great success, he now has a confident can-do spirit. "So many times when you try to do something in science, when you try to invent something, people tell you that it's impossible, that it will never work. But I think that is very rarely true. I think if you really believe in yourself, if you really stick to things, there is very little that is really impossible."[6]

Langer is not alone in personifying persistence at BPEC. Harvey Lodish continues to research and teach. He now leads an updated version of the course he and Wang designed in 1986, with Griffith as his teaching partner. Lauffenburger became the head of the Biological Engineering Department in 1998 and continues to lead it today. Griffith's grit includes her personal fight with cancer. She is now overseeing a roughly $30 million, five-year grant from the National Institutes of Health and the Defense Advanced Research Projects Agency (DARPA) to develop the *body on a chip*. In effect, Griffith and colleagues will build an in vitro system of multiple artificial organs to better study complex diseases.

The *body on a chip* project amounts to a third decade in which BPEC researchers are living the concept of Channeled Curiosity. Although BPEC has formally ceased operations, Griffith sees her NIH-DARPA grant as a direct descendent of BPEC. In the new project, she and her team are directing their energies to solve illnesses such as endometriosis, a painful disease that affects 10 percent of women and often causes infertility. Rather than merely experimenting from curiosity, the scientists are determined to put the *body on a chip* to good use. "It's not just building this physical thing. It's really rationally understanding how to get information out of it and how to model a complex human disease," Griffith says.

## CHALLENGES ASSOCIATED WITH CHANNELED CURIOSITY

Despite its great potential, there are risks associated with Channeled Curiosity. Among the greatest is that commercial concerns can corrupt research and the overall mission of universities to serve the public good. That is, commercial considerations on the part of university leaders or individual scholars can guide research projects toward ones that may promise riches but fail to solve pressing societal problems. Or self-interest, such as a desire to build a successful company, may influence investigators to conceal results or concoct false ones. In addition, the post–Bayh-Dole focus on patents and licenses raises a fundamental dilemma: Can universities balance the imperative to advance knowledge with the commercial desire to protect intellectual property?

Research guided by the Channeled Curiosity principle also can become too narrow or too product oriented. Solar cell company Solyndra, which filed for bankruptcy in 2011 after receiving a $535 million US Energy Department loan guarantee, offers a cautionary tale. For many observers, the case showed that government should not "pick winners" in the economy. We agree, in the sense that the government financing for Solyndra amounted to picking a company rather than "picking platforms," as we advocate.

Solyndra had a novel approach to photovoltaic cells, making them in the shape of tubes rather than flat panels. But its failure to thrive amid a price drop in standard solar cells indicates the perils of betting on a particular firm and its products rather than an underlying technology platform that may be adopted by a multitude of companies. Overly narrow research targets not only threaten to waste public money, they can also undermine the quality of research. In other words, too many restrictions placed on scientists can extinguish or at least diminish their sense of intellectual adventure. They can drive away the most talented investigators.

A related risk is red tape. ERCs and other research centers like them must be careful not to put too many planning and reporting requirements on scholars. Bureaucracy can smother creative sparks. Harvey Lodish, for example, questions the value of the planning process in the ERC model. To him, research that aims to solve real-world problems is just "doing good science." But the "good science" that Lodish and his colleagues have done comes in the context of a university that is among the world's best when it comes to channeling curiosity toward practical aims. Lodish and other engaged MIT scholars may not be able to recognize the supportive culture that surrounds them, and how it differs dramatically from other universities that do little to strategically plan to make a difference.

More generally, we are confident that more-practical research efforts can steer clear of overly narrow projects and head toward platform-oriented efforts. And that curiosity can be channeled in ways that inspire scholars. To repeat the words of former Bell Labs researcher and later US Energy Secretary Steven Chu, a climate of applied science like Bell Labs "doesn't destroy a kernel of genius, it focuses the mind."[7]

With respect to questions of commercial–academic compatibility, the tensions are centuries old and will never disappear completely. But the risks can be mitigated. Independent research committees can serve as watchdogs with respect to overall university research priorities. Policies can also reduce the chances that a particular professor will doctor or hide data. Disclosure rules at many institutions require scholars to acknowledge their business interests and consulting work, thereby making possible conflicts of interest clear. MIT also has a rule that a professor cannot own stock in a company that awards that professor a research grant.

Apart from policies, there is a deeper set of priorities that can preserve universities' integrity. Even as they emphasize high-impact research projects, they must keep education and the pursuit of knowledge as their top priorities. Here is how former MIT President Charles Vest described Robert Langer's approach to applied scholarship: "In my view, this style of research should be encouraged and enabled, but not expected. It should never become a primary goal or expectation of our faculty, and financial flows from such activities should not be integral to the financial plans and budgets of a university."[8] Langer agrees that a more practical, entrepreneurial mindset should be strictly voluntary at universities.[9] He also defends the way he has blended an academic career with an eye on real-world, commercial prospects. "I don't think I've lost much," he says. "I think I've gained more than I've lost." In other words, channeling his energies toward problems with a broader impact has not blinded him so much as opened his eyes to big possibilities. His point is in keeping with growing calls for universities to do more to direct their resources to solve problems.

## ENTREPRENEURIAL SHARP MINDS

In their recent book *Engines of Innovation*, authors Holden Thorp and Buck Goldstein say universities should embrace entrepreneurial thinking. By entrepreneurial, they mean not strictly a business mentality. But harkening back to the original definition of the term—to take action—they urge universities to be more willing to engage with the world, to be willing to fail, to get out of their comfort zones. And, they argue, universities do not have to lose their souls along the way. According to Thorp and Goldstein, "academics still too often equate entrepreneurship with opportunism or commercialization in a pejorative way. We see entrepreneurship as fully consonant with the aims of the modern university, in all its many and varied parts."[10]

So do we. We believe the Channeled Curiosity concept helps clarify how universities can act more entrepreneurially. The concept also steers us in the direction of better returns on our public research investments. Channeled Curiosity ensures that some of our greatest minds focus on improving society—with results such as medical breakthroughs and commercial technologies that boost the economy.

Griffith is among those sharp minds. In 2006, she earned a MacArthur "genius" award in part for her artificial liver work. And then BPEC's own research helped keep her productive when she herself was stricken with cancer. Thanks to Neulasta—and the Channeled Curiosity behind it—she hardly skipped a beat. "I ran my lab. I published papers. I even traveled because of that drug," she says. Although Griffith is a certifiable "genius," BPEC's success in enabling new drugs like Neulasta was not the product of academic geniuses working in isolation. On the contrary, as the BPEC record shows, collaborating with diverse colleagues inside and outside of academia was central to the Center's achievements. In the next chapter, we focus on the importance of such Boundary-Breaking Collaboration for technology breakthroughs.

## NOTES

1. Stokes, *Pasteur's Quadrant*.
2. Langer, "Enabling Scientific Innovation."
3. Ramanujam, Venkatraman, and Camillus, "Multi-Objective Assessment."

4. National Aeronautics and Space Administration, "Reliving the Wright Way."
5. Carswell, "Build a Liver."
6. Bowen et al., "Langer Lab," 13.
7. Gertner, "True Innovation."
8. Bowen et al., "Langer Lab," 6.
9. Langer also takes issue with MIT's policy on stock ownership and grants from companies. He would prefer simply to require scholars to disclose all their business interests.
10. Thorp and Goldstein, *Engines of Innovation*, 6.

# CHAPTER 6
# Boundary-Breaking Collaboration

For an academic, Kim Stelson is plainspoken. The University of Minnesota professor of engineering sums up his interests and background in four words: "I'm a controls guy." That simple phrase, though, packs in a lot of complexity. What Stelson means is that he specializes in concepts and technologies for monitoring and managing systems. He earned his doctorate at MIT with a focus on manufacturing process controls, which are used for such products as machinery that forms metal for automobiles. Later, Stelson shifted his attention to fluid power controls, and the optimal ways to regulate hydraulics like those found in car brakes and in a wide range of other machines that rely on high-pressure liquids or gases to do their jobs.

What the term *controls* also implies is that Stelson and others in his field are, by definition, *boundary spanners*. That is, they almost invariably have expertise and interests that bridge more than one traditional academic field. Control technology is not a conventional discipline like physics, math, or electrical engineering. An understanding of physical forces, machine parameters, and computer science must be stitched together to create successful controls. Stelson also takes boundary spanning a step further than some of his peers in academia. Although he has taught at the University of Minnesota since 1981, he has maintained an ongoing dialogue with the private sector. Most of his research in the 1980s and early 1990s was informed and funded by industry, including such corporate heavyweights as Boeing, Alcoa, General Electric, and General Motors. But as big US manufacturers began pulling back from basic research efforts, Stelson found it increasingly difficult to secure research contracts in the automotive, aerospace, and aluminum industries. Beginning in the mid-1990s, he decided to concentrate his efforts on the less-high-profile field of fluid power. Still, Stelson has continued his practices of knitting together different disciplines and forging connections between academia and industry. To this end, he spearheaded an effort to establish a NSF-funded Engineering Research Center focused on fluid power and became its founding director in 2006. The Center for Compact and Efficient Fluid Power (CCEFP), like all ERCs, draws from a range of scholarly fields and has deep ties to industry as it pursues its mission to develop the next generation of fluid power technologies.

Stelson's center has made progress in a field that is both quiet and crucial. Hydraulics and pneumatics are not seen as sexy, but they underpin modern industrial life—meaning, more efficient fluid power machines can make a big dent in the planet's pollution levels—and promise intriguing new applications. For example, CCEFP researchers developed a system for storing energy in the form of compressed air—technology that could breathe new life into the possibilities of wind power. Center researchers also have patented and built initial versions of an ankle orthosis that senses the motion of the wearer and aids them in walking. And other researchers have developed an energy-efficient excavator prototype that consumes about half the fuel of a standard digging truck. As Stelson puts it: "We gave a shot in the arm to mechanical engineering. I know that all the heavy equipment manufacturers are looking at our energy-efficient excavator."

Vital to the success is the way the center has broken through typical scholarly and institutional silos. Researchers associated with the center have expertise in fields ranging from biomedical engineering and mechanical engineering to machine design, robotics, and aging. These roughly thirty professors and sixty graduate students involve seven universities, including Georgia Tech, Purdue, Vanderbilt University, and the University of Illinois at Urbana-Champaign. Fifty private sector companies also participate in the center, including heavy-equipment makers Caterpillar and John Deere, industrial manufacturers Parker Hannifin and Eaton, and chemical companies Lubrizol and ExxonMobil. In addition, the center is consciously global: among its international partners are firms from Japan and Germany.

Collaboration across boundaries is not always easy. Scholars can be leery of working with researchers in other fields and other institutions, and may have difficulties communicating across disciplines. Meanwhile, private sector company officials can be harsh in their criticism of academic research as well as impatient with the pace of scholarship. There can be sticky questions about intellectual property. But straddling the various boundaries is worth it. We found this in our research of ERCs overall: inventors were more likely to generate patents in climates that fostered boundary spanning in terms of specific research projects, broader research areas, and academic disciplines. The importance of boundary spanning is no surprise to Kim Stelson. In fact, he cites the industry–university ties at his center as among the key factors to its real-world successes. "Working with industry is challenging, but in the end it means your research can have a great impact."

Stelson and his colleagues at the Center for Compact and Efficient Fluid Power embody the principle of *Boundary-Breaking Collaboration*, the second pillar of the Organized Innovation framework. Along with the other two "Cs" of the Organized Innovation framework—Channeled Curiosity and Orchestrated Commercialization—Boundary-Breaking Collaboration is a crucial ingredient in our formula for fostering technology breakthroughs. The remainder of this chapter focuses on defining Boundary-Breaking Collaboration, discussing our findings on the power of such cooperation, explaining how it can be put into place, illustrating the concept with examples, and addressing its possible drawbacks.


## DEFINING BOUNDARY-BREAKING COLLABORATION

*Boundary-Breaking Collaboration refers to facilitating information flow and collaboration among individuals representing different disciplines and perspectives in an effort to make new research discoveries more innovative.* The main boundaries in question are traditional academic disciplines as well as institutional boundaries, especially those between universities and between universities and private sector companies or government entities.

As we define it, Boundary-Breaking Collaboration affects multiple stages along the commercialization pipeline. That is, collaboration can help spark initial insights and discoveries by bringing together individuals with diverse perspectives. It also plays a role in the development of nascent technology and in the creation of working prototypes that can be tested with early feedback from academics of varied fields or industry players. In addition, boundary-spanning teamwork can improve the commercialization of the technology, as we will discuss in chapter 7. Including researchers in discussions with manufacturing employees and managers increasingly is seen as critical for accelerating advances and competitiveness. Innovation may take a linear or nonlinear form, but Boundary-Breaking Collaboration is almost invariably a critical catalyst.

In chapter 3, we discussed the fallacy of the myth of the individual genius. Citing the work of authors such as Malcolm Gladwell, Andrew Hargadon, and Ben Jones, we noted collaboration is vital to technological break-throughs for reasons including the growing complexity of knowledge and the effectiveness of brokering technologies from one realm to another. Other research has shown that crossing boundaries—creating what is called *organizational porosity*—tends to improve information flow.[1] Increased access to information, simply put, enhances innovation potential.

## A CLIMATE OF SUPPORT FOR COLLABORATION

The ERC program has produced a great amount of Boundary-Breaking Collaboration over the years. Medical researchers have teamed up with electrical engineers. Computer scientists have joined forces with college campus security officials. Physiologists have worked with chemical and environmental engineers. And academics have routinely worked with industry leaders. Still, our research found that not all ERCs had the same effectiveness with respect to Boundary-Breaking Collaboration. The differences in the degree to which the centers encouraged Boundary-Breaking Collaboration played a large role in how productive they were in terms of commercialization activity. Our research on ERCs reveals that fostering a boundary-spanning organizational climate is key to patent generation.

What do we mean by a boundary-spanning organizational climate? Simply put, organizational climate reflects shared employee perceptions of the organizational context.[2] Climate is important because it represents formal policies and procedures as well as informal social norms, which let us know what is expected in a particular organizational context.[3] Organizational climate can be a powerful influence on behavior. Our analysis of the ERCs showed that researchers are more likely to generate patents in climates that cultivate boundary spanning across research projects, research areas, and academic disciplines. In particular, innovative ideas that cross these boundaries in an ERC are more likely to be novel and influenced by diverse viewpoints, thus they are more likely to receive a patent award.[4] Spanning boundaries can also help researchers generate more ideas, cross-pollinate their ideas in different research areas, obtain feedback from multiple perspectives, and test new technologies in various research domains. In support of this, one ERC leader said the "multidisciplinary effect [in the ERC] has been great for idea generation."

This effect of boundary-spanning climate may take time. In our examination, we surveyed employees about organizational climate and, two years later, we assessed the benefits of climate. But we also found the benefits of boundary-spanning climate exceeded the benefits of a climate that generally promotes and supports commercialization or the benefits of simply having many financial resources. More discussion of commercialization support follows in chapter 7.

In our analyses, we found patent awards were thirty times more likely to occur in an ERC where participants "Strongly Agreed" their climate was characterized by boundary spanning as compared with a climate where participants merely "Agreed" their climate was boundary spanning.


## HOW TO BREAK BOUNDARIES

How do university leaders create a climate of Boundary-Breaking Collaboration? Our study of ERCs and other research on technology commercialization suggest a six-point formula. The first two points focus on management processes; the last four represent boundaries that should be purposely crossed.

- Lead through persuasion and trust
- Create interdependence
- Promote collaboration across academic disciplines
- Connect with industry
- Link universities
- Seek active dialogue with government representatives


### Lead through Persuasion and Trust

Successful Boundary-Breaking Collaboration starts with leading through persuasion and trust. Leaders in academia, business, and government increasingly face a reality defined by ad hoc projects, globally dispersed teams, and flatter organizational structures. Hierarchical management methods—command-and-control approaches—are disappearing. The emerging leadership models tend to emphasize persuasion, influence, and listening. If anything, these trends requiring influential management are more pronounced in research centers embracing Organized Innovation.

For instance, those spearheading Organized Innovation efforts must be able to span boundaries. They need to speak the languages of both industry and academia. Perhaps most important is that leaders be able to persuade people of the benefits of collaboration. They must understand the technology well enough to talk about big picture goals as well as detailed experiments and technical challenges associated with the research. They also must be able to manage complex projects effectively, which typically requires the ability to solve problems creatively.

Leaders must also inspire trust, which is vital to the flow of ideas and information to different people and institutions.[5] For example, in our observations of ERC leaders, we perceived that those who can build trust benefit their centers because increased trust leads to improved information flow, more cooperative agreements, and decreased transaction costs. It is easier to execute transactions when participants are required to work together.[6] Those consequences of greater trust lead to more innovation success.[7]

## Create Interdependence

Leaders can influence the level of Boundary-Breaking Collaboration simply in the ways they map out their research plan. By integrating projects and promoting interdependence among the research thrusts and individual scholars, leaders can stimulate more boundary spanning. One ERC leader told us his center had a research structure that hindered boundary spanning: "We can't get collaboration ERC-wide because of a wide breadth of research topics and structure." But other ERC leaders designed their research goals and plans to maximize the interaction among different sorts of scholars. Several told us they "encourage [boundary-crossing] teamwork by making funding decisions based on the collaborative nature of a project" and "give priority to cross-discipline projects." Another said that research "thrusts are designed to force interdependence and, therefore, collaboration."

Just as our research found that promoting interdependence was a vital ingredient to productive collaboration in university-based research centers, there is increased appreciation of the concept in the business world. Interdependence has been found to be a critical factor to high-performance sales teams.[8] Research on some 2,600 IBM employees found that more socially connected workers were better performing than their peers. The value of this "social capital" could be quantified—on average, every e-mail contact was worth an added $948 in revenue for the company.[9] Both companies and university-based research centers can use interdependence to promote Boundary-Breaking Collaboration.

The above points focused on generic leadership processes. The next four involve specific organizational boundaries to be crossed to achieve true Boundary-Breaking Collaboration.

## Promote Collaboration across Academic Disciplines

The first boundary to be bridged is the one that separates academic disciplines. As we have noted earlier, the most groundbreaking innovations often emerge at the intersections of different areas of expertise. Researchers we interviewed at ERCs repeatedly mentioned the value of considering distinct viewpoints from people in other disciplines. This diversity of input is critical in pursuing highly complex and ambitious research. Research centers, therefore, must promote cooperation and connections among researchers from a variety of fields.

Leaders can persuade colleagues to break out of academic silos through speeches, conversations, and introductions. This *academic bully pulpit* approach can be reinforced by selecting ambitious projects that all but require diverse researchers to team up and that inspire them to do so. ERCs featured such mechanisms as committees that monitored collaboration; researchers who coordinated across thrusts; and mentoring between senior faculty, junior faculty, and students. Incentives help, too. ERCs entice scholars of different stripes to join forces by offering significant funding if they do. Other carrots can be used to foster a culture of interdisciplinary cooperation. For example, university leaders can work to supplement the traditional academic researcher incentive structure with rewards for commercialization outputs such as invention disclosures, patents, and licenses. Or multidisciplinary publications might be encouraged for tenure and promotion decisions, in addition to single-discipline publications.

## Connect with Industry

Another boundary to cross is the one separating industry and universities. In general, relationships between academic faculty and companies foster more patents, licenses, and spin-off firm success.[10] At ERCs, more interaction between center representatives and industry partners is associated with more relevant research because of input about market demand from industry experts or entrepreneurs.[11] We found that the most impressive ERCs place strong value on collaborating with industry partners, and these relationships with industry are carefully defined to encourage widespread information sharing regarding research progress and industry needs.

Research centers can spur industry–academia cooperation in part through directives. The ERC program, for example, requires centers to bring in industry members and to create an industry advisory board that helps set research strategy. But requirements alone are not enough to generate meaningful exchanges between scholars and the private sector. Another crucial factor is a hospitable university atmosphere that offers benefits for the industry partners; in ERCs these benefits include well-trained graduates as employees and access to cutting-edge information.

As one ERC member put it, the general approach of his university was "nonconfrontational and more cooperative with industry." An ERC feature that helps promote positive collaboration with the private sector is the industrial liaison officer (ILO). This post goes a step beyond the typical university office of technology transfer. ILOs, often people with experience in both academia and industry, play a key role in creating and nurturing relationships with companies that can help steer research in more promising directions. We discuss the ILO role in more detail in chapter 7.

## Link Universities

A third category of boundaries involves the interfaces among universities. Forging ties across universities can reap benefits including new, productive collaborations among complementary scholars, increased access to specialized equipment, and wider networks of industry ties that can improve research relevance. The ERCs are showcases of the power of linking universities together. For example, the Georgia Tech/Emory Center for the Engineering of Living Tissues advances tissue engineering technology for purposes including organ transplants. The center produced several successful start-ups and was itself a product of an existing partnership between Georgia Tech and Emory. The Wallace H. Coulter Department of Biomedical Engineering at Georgia Tech and Emory University was created jointly by the Emory University School of Medicine and the Georgia Tech College of Engineering. In 2012, *U.S. News & World Report* ranked the department's undergraduate and graduate programs second in the nation in biomedical engineering.

Research cooperation involving multiple institutions is a growing trend.[12] But how best to do it? Enticing universities with funding earmarked for cross-institution collaboration is one strategy. It also can help to make each partner university put "skin in the game" by having to contribute matching funds to joint initiatives. Communication is vital, in that center officials at different schools need to share ideas and updates frequently. Also crucial for inter-university cooperation is support from high-level administrators such as university presidents/chancellors, provosts, and deans.

### Seek Active Dialogue with Government Representatives

A final key boundary is that separating universities and government officials. Universities already engage with government to secure grant funding for research initiatives. But leaders may find themselves at a competitive advantage if they take a more proactive, partnership approach. That is, even before requests for proposals are written and published by government agencies, university leaders and their industry partners can help government officials understand the most pressing needs for large-scale research initiatives. We are not suggesting special treatment or lobbyist-style influence tactics, but rather long-term partnerships through which government agencies stay attuned to societal needs and the current research landscape. Government agencies may find they are funding more high-potential innovation initiatives when they foster this type of ongoing dialogue.

We also suggest that university–government dialogue continue in a long-term coaching relationship. When government representatives act as coach or mentor of institutions that follow Organized Innovation principles, they become a more active participant in ensuring its success. Government entities have exposure to their diverse portfolio of investments, and some of these investments pay off better than others. They should look for and share the key differences in how those research initiatives are executed; these best practices can and should be shared in a coaching capacity by government leaders responsible for overseeing those research programs. University leaders might proactively seek such information when it is not provided; government representatives, particularly those that participate in accountability assessments of ERCs and similar centers, are untapped sources of such information. Government representatives can also facilitate collaboration among leaders of similar research centers to share such best practices and lessons learned.

Having defined Boundary-Breaking Collaboration and spelled out a formula to achieve it, let's examine the concept in action. A closer look at the Center for Compact and Effective Fluid Power shows the power of cooperation that breaks through boundaries that often constrain science and engineering research.

## BOUNDARY-BREAKING COLLABORATION AT THE CENTER FOR COMPACT AND EFFICIENT FLUID POWER

In general, ERCs demonstrate a high level of collaboration. As large-scale research endeavors that explicitly require cooperation involving different academic disciplines, multiple universities, and industry partners, ERCs typically prompt boundary crossing from project conception through the later stages of the commercialization pipeline. Many people we interviewed in our research felt their ERC had institutionalized a broader collaboration mentality than they would otherwise experience. For instance, ERC participants told us that an advantage of the stable funding provided by the ERC program is that it offers "increased flexibility for additional collaboration over a longer timeline" and "a framework for collaboration among people that want to." Another leader said faculty members working in ERCs enjoy the "learning potential involved in collaborating with multiple disciplines, which leads to new ways of thinking and whole new paradigms." All the collaboration has an impact; more than one researcher emphasized that more nontraditional boundary spanning had a noticeable influence on ERC output.

At CCEFP, outputs such as the high efficiency excavator have garnered attention. The center's success, in fact, is largely a function of widespread, varied, cooperative efforts. At the root of CCEFP's collaborative culture is center director Kim Stelson. To a great extent, he personifies the principle of leading through persuasion and trust. He set up the vision of the center, demonstrating that the ostensibly dull field of fluid power was full of exciting possibilities. Stelson convinced colleagues at the University of Minnesota and other universities to join him on an ambitious quest to transform the field with less-polluting equipment; novel safe, clean, and quiet power systems; and a new generation of human-scale machines such as the ankle orthosis. Together, he and his team came up with a bold set of aims: that fluid power efficiency in transportation could be doubled, that the ability of fluid power systems to store energy could jump by a factor of ten, and that new hydraulic and pneumatic systems could shrink in size by ten to twenty times.[13]

Although they were bold goals, Stelson and his colleagues made a strong case that each was achievable in the course of activities of a ten-year research center. They won over NSF officials, who granted them funding to start the center. Similarly, center leaders attracted some fifty industry partners, including major players in the various fields touching fluid power, such as petrochemicals and heavy equipment manufacturing.

One of the ways that Stelson and his leadership team have fostered trust among these many players is through transparent communication. Every other week the center features a webcast for researchers associated with different projects to share progress and dilemmas. The presentations— often made by graduate students and postdoctoral researchers—attract more than scholars alone. Member company employees also regularly participate in the calls.

CCEFP also has fostered Boundary-Breaking Collaboration by consciously creating interdependence. Like all ERCs, it established a set of research thrusts and test beds that collectively prompt researchers to work together. The center's three thrusts of *efficiency*, *effectiveness*, and *compactness* involve roughly thirty research projects that often link up in one or more of the center's four test beds: the high-efficiency excavator, a hydraulic-hybrid passenger vehicle, a compact rescue robot, and a fluid-powered ankle-foot orthosis. By itself, the orthosis test bed weaves in noise and vibration control research from one professor, compact air compressor power from another, and new, smaller valves from a third. The ankle-foot orthosis, for which a patent application was filed in 2010, has the potential to help millions of people in the United States alone who are affected by stroke, polio, and multiple sclerosis, not to mention people with ankle joint injuries.

As with all ERCs, cross-disciplinary work has been built into the center's various projects. Among the most productive cases of cooperation by scholars from different academic backgrounds is the research team of University of Minnesota professors Perry Li and Jim Van de Ven. Li, like Kim Stelson, is a controls specialist. He has a background in electrical and information sciences, and worked a stint as a researcher at Xerox. Van de Ven, by contrast, is the more mechanical of the pair. His specialty has been machine design, including the creation of a suspension system for a new snowmobile. That focus has to do with his upbringing in rural Minnesota. "I grew up as a farm kid," he says, "always tinkering with things."

They have brought their talents together to create a novel accumulator design, one that has proven to offer twenty times the energy storage density of traditional hydraulic systems. Typical accumulators rely on enclosed chambers to store gas, and as a fluid is pumped into the chamber—driven, say, by the act of braking a car—the pressure of the gas increases and can later be used to drive a motor as the gas expands. But the energy capacity, or density, of such systems is limited by the size of the chamber and its need to contain the gas and fluid volumes. Van de Ven and Li's *open accumulator* design sidesteps this barrier by connecting the chamber to the atmosphere. During the storage phase, valves and pistons draw air from the atmosphere into the chamber. During the subsequent "motoring" phase of turning compressed air into power, air can be expelled into the atmosphere. The new design amounts to a breakthrough in fluid power efficiency. It required the skills of both Li, who worked out complex algorithms to control the chamber valves, and Van de Ven, who imagined the more complex machinery involved and built a working proof of concept.

Initially, Li and Van de Ven planned for their upgraded accumulator to fit into passenger vehicles. But even with the more efficient open accumulator design, the accumulator needed for a car driven in typical start-and-stop fashion would be so big that "it would take up the entire back seat," as Stelson puts it. So Li and Van de Van shifted gears. They realized that wind power might be better suited to their technology, given the consistent, slow turn of big turbines. Storing energy in open accumulators built into the foundations of turbines or nearby them could help solve the problem of power grids not built to accept low-voltage transmissions. The accumulators can potentially collect wind energy to the point that it can be sent at the voltage level appropriate for current power lines. They are likely to be cheaper than electrochemical batteries of the same scale. To date, renewable wind energy has been more expensive than traditional energy sources. But Van de Ven and Li's technology raises the prospect that wind energy "becomes viable now," Stelson says.

Two companies focusing on energy storage have licensed the open accumulator technology: SustainX and LightSail Energy. LightSail, in particular, is gaining notice in the clean energy arena. In late 2012, it announced it had raised $37.3 million in funding from investors including Bill Gates, PayPal co-founder Peter Thiel, and prominent venture capital firm Khosla Ventures. In addition, Li and Van de Ven have won a separate NSF grant to pursue the technology.

CCEFP also has demonstrated a great deal of collaboration between academia and the private sector. Purdue University engineering professor Monika Ivantysynova, for example, worked with industry to demonstrate a dramatically more efficient hydraulic excavator. Ivantysynova and her research team overhauled a standard compact excavator donated by Bobcat. The standard design for excavators and other heavy equipment is a central hydraulic pump that has to be powerful enough to handle the most taxing jobs, such as lifting heavy concrete pipe sections. But a big central pump generates more energy than is needed for smaller tasks, such as rotating the digging arm. To accomplish lesser jobs smoothly and safely, valves give off excess energy, and roughly 40 percent of a typical excavator's fuel energy is wasted this way. Replacing the central pump with smaller modular ones and using pumps that can vary their size depending on pressure needs reaped big energy savings. Ivantysynova's group also built in a version of the regenerative braking that can be found in electric hybrid cars. In performance tests managed by Caterpillar, the CCEFP's experimental excavator uses roughly 50 percent less energy than a typical excavator.

Ivantysynova also worked with industrial manufacturer Parker Hannifin on a hydraulic hybrid drive train system for trucks. Hydraulic hybrid vehicles offer similar fuel efficiency gains as electric hybrids. But hydraulic technology is a better option for hybrid trucks and larger vehicles, because hydraulic hybrids have better "power density" than electric ones. In other words, the battery needed to handle heavy-duty tasks in an electric hybrid delivery truck is massive. Beginning around 2008, Parker Hannifin asked Ivantysynova to extend the hydraulic hybrid transmission technology the company had created for garbage trucks. Three years later, she and her students delivered a new transmission concept. The resulting drive train—which includes the engine, transmission, hydraulic systems, and electronic controls—is lighter, smaller, and ideally suited for delivery vehicles. Parker Hannifin's hydraulic hybrid technology, including contributions from Ivantysynova's lab, was so promising that the company opened a new manufacturing factory outside of Columbus, Ohio, to produce the systems. Roughly 100 jobs were created at the new division. Parker Hannifin is now shipping systems installed in refuse trucks and delivery vehicles used by companies including UPS and FedEx.

CCEFP also incorporates extensive inter-university collaboration. Following the ERC model that requires a host university to team up with other schools, its formal partners are the University of Minnesota, Georgia Tech, Purdue, the University of Illinois at Urbana-Champaign, Milwaukee School of Engineering, North Carolina A&T State University, and Vanderbilt University. This is not a partnership in name only. As mentioned above, the ankle-foot orthosis project alone involves multiple universities. The biweekly webcast helps researchers at the various schools connect and share information, and ad hoc workshops and meetings span university boundaries. Hosting CCEFP's annual meeting rotates among the partner universities.

Stelson and other leaders at CCEFP have established an active conversation with government officials. As at all ERCs, center leaders are responsible for generating an annual report of their activities for NSF, and for hosting an annual site visit for NSF representatives. In addition, all ERCs have extensive reviews at years three and six to assess the program's performance and strategy and determine whether funding should continue in subsequent years. At CCEFP's six-year review in 2012, NSF officials expressed dissatisfaction with the center's plan for the future. CCEFP was put on what amounts to probation—its leaders had one year to better justify continued government investment in the center. Stelson concedes NSF's criticism was fair. He says he and his team focused too much on past accomplishments rather than upcoming research directions and technology transfer milestones. In this sense, the constant dialogue between the CCEFP and government leaders helps to optimize the use of public research dollars. Stelson is determined to get it right the next time around. "I'm expecting to get renewed," he says. In fact, they were renewed.

## CHALLENGES ASSOCIATED WITH BOUNDARY-BREAKING COLLABORATION

CCEFP's experience shows that it is not always easy to manage such large-scale collaboration. Stelson says he wishes he had received more training in this area. "Strategic planning and project management are really important skills for managing these projects," he says. His point is well taken. It is not trivial for academics familiar with managing at most several graduate students and research budgets of several hundred thousand dollars to take on the leadership of centers pursuing Organized Innovation at a significant scale. Such centers may involve a multimillion-dollar budget and an organization that encompasses multiple academic disciplines, several universities, private sector companies, and, in the case of the ERCs, one or more economic development organizations, middle schools, and high schools.

The difficulty of managing complex research centers is one of several challenges associated with Boundary-Breaking Collaboration. A related one centers on the possibility that research projects can get bogged down by bureaucracy. We heard such concerns in our research into ERCs. ERC leaders are required to assemble and write lengthy annual reports, and many found these reporting requirements too taxing.

Leaders of university-based research centers also may face significant mistrust or skepticism as they try to break down boundaries for improved research collaboration. Suspicions may exist between faculty members in the same department, between faculty members of different departments, and between faculty and industry representatives. Apart from trust issues, there is the challenge of getting different parties to communicate effectively—to speak a common language. Many ERC participants we interviewed commented that "industry has no philosophy in how to work with universities" and "universities need to learn to work with industry and vice versa." A related hurdle in bringing industry together with academia is that companies may be skittish about exposing their views and strategies in a room full of their rivals.

Boundary-Breaking Collaboration efforts can raise ethical dilemmas. For example, a more permeable relationship between the private sector and professors leads to concerns that academic freedom and pursuit of knowledge for the public good could be compromised. Research sponsored directly by companies, in particular, carries risks. Scholars may produce biased findings. Or conclusions damaging to companies could be buried in ways that harm the public.[14] In a less sinister way, close collaboration between academics and industry can lead research to become overly "applied" and incremental as scholars focus more on companies' immediate needs rather than long-term, groundbreaking innovations.

These are legitimate concerns; however, we believe all can be addressed or mitigated. Oversight can be arranged so that industry-guided research does not become overly narrow or come at the expense of curiosity-driven research that serves the common good. Such oversight could come in the form of NSF reviews or those of faculty advisory boards. Guidelines similar to those of the ERCs—which specify that basic science and engineering topics be explored and oriented toward commercialization—help guarantee that faculty will continue to play their historical role of fundamental discovery even as they seek to solve real-world problems.

To prevent the problem of research suppression, membership agreements with industry can be based on the principle that the publication of results can be temporarily postponed but not prevented. That is, private sector firms sponsoring research with center faculty might legitimately expect scholars to delay publication of results for a reasonable period so that patents can be filed or a technology tested further. But findings must not remain proprietary forever.

The difficulty of bringing industry rivals to the same table can be overcome by targeting research on very early-stage investigations that nonetheless have great commercial potential. The high-efficiency excavator is a case in point, because its modular design and other advances represent a new platform rather than a particular product that competitors will fight over.

Despite the challenge of translating among different camps and overcoming the mistrust they may have of each other, it can be done. High-integrity people must be chosen as leaders to set a trustworthy tone at the top. Center leaders should also be familiar with the perspectives and concerns of different disciplines, and with both academia and industry. Stelson and Brad Bohlmann of CCEFP are good examples of leaders with broad experience and the ability to talk to many different kinds of people.

Red-tape concerns are real in Boundary-Breaking Collaboration and Organized Innovation overall. Leaders and government overseers must be careful to balance the need for ongoing accountability with reasonable documentation and evaluation requirements. For example, we believe annual reviews of research centers practicing Boundary-Breaking Collaboration should have a coaching orientation rather than a purely evaluative one. Critical reviews involving comprehensive reporting on center activities could be reserved for assessing the centers at years three and six.

Developing leaders capable of managing extensive collaborative research efforts also is a significant challenge. One way NSF has sought to help ERC directors learn skills associated with fostering effective collaboration is through an annual conference that includes leaders from all ERCs. What is more, center leaders over the years have compiled a Best Practices Manual. We believe a mandatory training session for center directors on topics including strategic planning and project management would be a helpful addition to the ERC program and a necessary component for other such research initiatives.

Although they have room for improvement, ERCs and centers like them act implicitly as training grounds for the skills needed to lead highly collaborative research programs. Every time graduate students, postdocs, and professors present their findings to colleagues from other disciplines and members of industry, they are improving their ability to communicate with a wider audience. Their exposure to highly integrated research projects helps them see how to design such interdependent efforts in the future. Experiencing firsthand the power of joining forces with others beyond their academic specialty can transform them into advocates for Boundary-Breaking Collaboration.

## A BRIDGE FROM THE PAST TO THE FUTURE

Stelson, for example, sees his ERC as restoring some of the cooperation between industry and universities that he experienced decades ago. The professors, students, postdoctoral fellows, and corporate leaders collaborating through his center are forging professional bonds. Stelson says helping to make those connections for the younger generation of scholars is the most meaningful part of leading the center—a job that has challenged him more than any other in his career. "It's the most satisfying and the most difficult thing I've ever done," he says. "It provides me with an opportunity to create an environment where some of these young people can succeed."

Stelson's simple comment speaks volumes. In trying to reconstruct something of the climate that allowed him to thrive in his younger days, Stelson is not only serving the engineering researchers following in his footsteps but also the country that relies on the innovations they generate and the world that may benefit from those advances. In short, this community of broad-minded, boundary-breaking researchers holds the key to a better future. Next we turn to see how to ensure that the research of teams such as Stelson's will turn into products, companies, and whole new industries.

## NOTES

1. Adams, "Structure and Dynamics of Behavior"; Owen-Smith and Powell, "Expanding Role of University Patenting." See also Paul Nurse, Richard Treisman and Jim Smith, "Building Better Institutions," *Science*, 5 July 2013, Vol. 341, p. 10. Nurse, Treisman, and Smith talk about the importance of a research institution being "permeable to interactions with outside researchers and organizations."
2. Schneider, White, and Paul, "Linking Service Climate and Customer Perceptions."
3. Zohar and Luria, "Multilevel Model of Safety Climate."
4. Hunter, Perry, and Currall, "Inside Multi-Disciplinary Science and Engineering Research Centers."
5. Currall and Judge, "Measuring Trust."
6. Dyer and Wujin, "Role of Trustworthiness."
7. Perry, Currall, and Stuart, "Pipeline from University Laboratory"; Currall and Inkpen, "Complexity of Organizational Trust"; Currall and Epstein, "Fragility of Organizational Trust"; Clegg et al., "Implicating Trust."
8. Gap International, "Competition or Collaboration?"
9. Baker, "Putting a Price on Social Connections."
10. Thursby and Thursby, "Are Faculty Critical?"; Stuart, "Interorganizational Alliances"; Shane and Stuart, "Organizational Endowments"; Stuart and Ding, "When Do Scientists Become Entrepreneurs?"
11. Perry, Currall, and Stuart, "Pipeline from University Laboratory"; Feller, Ailes, and Roessner, "Impacts of Research Universities."
12. Hale, "Collaboration in Academic R&D."
13. Center for Compact and Efficient Fluid Power, "About Us."
14. Such concerns are not merely academic. Cases have surfaced in recent years where pharmaceutical companies, in particular, have been found to suppress research results. For example, Schering-Plough, maker of the cholesterol drug Vytorin, failed to disclose for two years the results of a clinical trial showing the drug provided no benefit in improving artery health. During that time, the drug was marketed to consumers in TV ads. See Fauber, "Drug Research Routinely Suppressed."

# CHAPTER 7

# Orchestrated Commercialization

To get a clear picture of the power of Orchestrated Commercialization, consider the case of Riccardo Santini. At age seventeen, Santini started losing his sight to retinitis pigmentosa, a disease that damages the eye tissue needed to convert light into nerve signals. The ailment gradually narrowed Santini's field of vision and blinded him completely by the time he was twenty-five. The Italian physiotherapist remained in the dark for thirty-six years. He became a father to a daughter, Elena. Then, a few years ago, Santini received one of the first artificial retinas designed by Mark Humayun. The device, dubbed the Argus II and produced by the firm Second Sight Medical Products, gained US FDA approval in early 2013, but was first approved in the European Union.

Essentially a bionic eye, the Argus II captures video from a camera embedded in eyeglasses and relays digital signals to an implant placed directly on the retina. The result is not a re-creation of human vision per se, but a second sight more akin to a video screen made of pixels. The low-resolution version of the Argus II given to Santini and other initial patients does not allow wearers to discern facial features. But when his implant was turned on, Santini nonetheless saw plenty. He vividly remembers the scene as physicians and Elena, now twenty-eight, awaited his reaction. "Doctors, for the first time in my life, I can see the shape of my daughter," he told those surrounding him. The brightness from overhead lights and sunlight coming through a window were no less wonderful to Santini: "Regaining sight of light is beautiful."

The benefits Santini and other patients have experienced from the Argus II echo biblical miracles. But this technology to enable blind people to see again is the product of human effort and ingenuity. The story of the Argus II is one of visionary leadership, interdisciplinary teamwork, and commercial savvy. It starts with research begun by Humayun twenty-five years ago, when his grandmother's blindness set him on a journey to help people like her. Humayun not only broadened his expertise to encompass medicine and engineering, he also assembled a team that included both fields. And at an early stage, he connected with the private sector, helping to form Second Sight with veteran medical device entrepreneur Alfred Mann.

Second Sight, as well as an early prototype of the artificial retina, came before Humayun spearheaded the creation of the Biomimetic MicroElectronic Systems (BMES) Engineering Research Center in 2003. But Humayun and other researchers at this University of Southern California based ERC were integral in organizing clinical trials of a Second Sight prototype. And BMES researchers have advanced the technology to the point that experimental versions of the device now allow patients to distinguish facial features, better read large print, and navigate more easily around furniture. Humayun and his team also began exploring the broader possibilities of electronic implants. They are now outlining a novel field of bioelectronics, one that could generate good American jobs even as it helps address maladies ranging from depression and short-term memory loss to bladder control problems and spinal paralysis.

Developing and commercializing groundbreaking technology like the artificial retina is not easy. Such projects typically demand years of perseverance—more than two decades' worth in the case of the Argus II. They require bridging the often-clashing cultures of academia and industry. They take a willingness to progress through the many steps to market, which may include filing for patents, hammering out technology licenses, searching for start-up funding, and working with regulatory agencies.

But as the artificial retina shows, it can be done. Research points to a number of best practices for managing the transfer of discoveries from university labs to living rooms. For example, our analyses of ERCs showed that centers with an organizational climate supporting commercialization were more likely to generate invention disclosures—which are declarations of discoveries that precede patents.

Leadership is a key ingredient in creating the right commercialization climate. Mark Humayun has stood out as particularly effective, resembling an orchestra conductor as he supervised the artificial retina's development. He has assembled a diverse set of complementary players, from academia and the private sector. He has coaxed them into working from the same score—a plan to create the artificial retina and related bioelectric devices. He also has prepared them to perform for the public, by developing commercially available products. Ultimately, he has led a team to make beautiful music together. Or to create beautiful moments, such as a father seeing his daughter for the first time and enjoying the sun's rays after three decades of darkness.

Humayun and the Biomimetic Microelectronic Systems ERC embody the principle of Orchestrated Commercialization. This principle is the third and final of the three pillars of Organized Innovation. Along with the other two "Cs"—Channeled Curiosity and Boundary-Breaking Collaboration—Orchestrated Commercialization is a vital element in our blueprint for generating technology breakthroughs. The rest of this chapter defines Orchestrated Commercialization, explains how to implement it, illustrates the principle with examples, and considers its challenges.

## DEFINING ORCHESTRATED COMMERCIALIZATION

*Orchestrated Commercialization refers to intentionally coordinating complementary players—researchers, patent officers, entrepreneurs, financial investors, and corporations—to maximize the success of the technology commercialization process.* Leaders must marshal the talents and inspire the work of various groups, forging productive connections among them. Orchestrated Commercialization means understanding and navigating the realms of science and engineering, intellectual property protection, technology licensing, start-ups, venture capital, and corporate product development. It means retaining a sharp focus not just on intriguing insights, but on translating them into real-world products and services.

Prioritizing the commercialization of federally funded research is gaining momentum amid calls for closer ties between universities and business.[1] A 2012 study by the President's Council of Advisors on Science and Technology (PCAST) concluded that, to enhance our economic competitiveness as a nation, universities should act as "central engines of innovation and geographical anchors of the Nation's science and technology enterprise."[2] The PCAST report also saw hopeful signs that such "hubs" have taken shape, stating:

> U.S. research universities are today performing not only the basic research for which they have been best known during the last 50 years, but to an increasing extent applied and translational research with the potential to deliver innovations, new industries, and market efficiencies over the next 50 years. Today, American research universities are closer to the marketplace than they have ever been, with a focus on translating and transferring research discoveries to industry.[3]

## A CLIMATE OF SUPPORT FOR COMMERCIALIZATION

The ERC program is a prime example of the way universities can serve as the nexus of innovation efforts by emphasizing the translation and transfer of research. That said, our research on ERCs discovered that some were more successful than others in generating commercialization outputs.

In chapter 6 we discussed the importance of a climate of Boundary-Breaking Collaboration in producing higher numbers of patents. Our research found a similar effect when it comes to the extent to which ERCs fostered a climate of support for commercialization. A climate that supports commercialization refers to shared beliefs in a group that practices, procedures, and behaviors promote the commercialization of technology. In effect, it is the shared sense that moving research discoveries into the real world is encouraged and that resources are available for these efforts.

In our examinations of ERCs, we found that invention disclosures were four times more likely in an ERC where participants "Strongly Agreed" that their climate supported commercialization compared with an ERC where participants merely "Agreed" that their climate supported commercialization. Most commercialization activity starts with invention disclosures, or declarations by researchers that they have generated a new discovery—an idea or object—that could be worthy of a patent. A strong commercialization support climate encourages scholars to make those formal declarations, taking the time to file the paperwork associated with them. Incentives and support structures are more likely to be in place in such a climate, leading to a dramatic impact on commercialization activity.

## HOW TO ORCHESTRATE COMMERCIALIZATION

So how should leaders of university-based research centers foster a climate of commercialization? And, more generally, how should they orchestrate commercialization? Our study of ERCs and other research on technology commercialization suggests a six-point formula for orchestrating commercialization.

- Coordinate the network
- Elevate role models
- Revisit incentives for commercializing academic research
- Appoint an industrial liaison officer
- Improve technology transfer and administrative execution
- Bring in entrepreneurial and business expertise

## Coordinate the Network

One of the most important leadership activities in Orchestrated Commercialization is coordinating the network of participants so that nascent technology will progress toward the commercial, public sphere. This is work of matchmaking, of connecting people and institutions and leveraging an innovation ecosystem. For example, professors with encouraging technical findings may need to hold conversations with researchers in adjacent fields, with officials in technology transfer offices, or with entrepreneurs to fully explore the possibilities of their discoveries. The researchers may require connections with skilled technicians or engineers to build a proof of concept or prototype. They may need to work with venture capitalists, corporations, or patent attorneys for the technology to move toward a marketable product. Orchestrating such relationships allows for the networking that authors Jeff Dyer, Hal Gregersen, and Clayton Christensen call vital to innovation, and for the brokering that Hargadon says lies at the heart of technology breakthroughs.[4]

Intentionally coordinating the network, though, is about more than just forging ties among players. Part of what makes those links lead to commercial progress is an inspiring vision. Related to the Channeled Curiosity component of Leading with Vision, a compelling mission motivates people to engage in the work of turning an intriguing insight into a proof of concept, filing the proper invention disclosures and patent applications, securing funding for a start-up, and manufacturing a product for consumers. Leaders able to articulate their vision in a "multilingual" way—in the vernacular of scientists, university administrators, investors, regulators, and the public—can overcome and reverse attitudes that often hinder academic–industry cooperation and commercialization.

## Elevate Role Models

Among the most powerful motivators for changing behavior is the presence of role models. This holds true for prodding scholars to become more passionate about technology commercialization.[5] The presence of peers who have launched a start-up that significantly addressed a public dilemma or that sold for $100 million—or both—inspires others in an academic department. It may also tap into competitive urges. Our research on ERCs found technology commercialization performance was affected by how often a researcher's department chair and other departmental members were themselves involved in commercialization activities. A critical mass of scholar-entrepreneurs at places like Stanford and MIT helps explain their continued success.

Many other universities have such individuals who can help shift a climate in the direction of technology commercialization, but they may not be well known to their university community. Finding such scholars and telling their stories through internal publications, and to the broader community through communications and marketing efforts, raises their profile—and increases their influence among peers. At universities with few professors who stand out for their accomplishments beyond academia, leaders can work to create role models from within by helping researchers achieve small wins through planning and support, and then celebrate those milestones publicly. It also may be necessary to hire professors who succeed both academically and commercially to achieve positive role model effects.

### Revisit Incentives for Commercializing Academic Research

The right rewards can do much to cultivate a climate that supports commercialization. We call for broadening traditional criteria considered in tenure and promotion decisions to include a scholar's work on interdisciplinary, ambitious projects and performance in bringing nascent technologies to the public. That's not to say that conventional measures such as publications in prestigious, peer-reviewed journals and advances within a specific academic discipline should be eliminated. But expanding the scope of scholarly success to encompass broader measures of research impact such as invention disclosures, patents, and policy advice would go a long way toward promoting behaviors that boost commercialization efforts. We discuss these themes further in chapter 8.

Apart from incentives related to career milestones, other carrots in the academic setting can encourage technology transfer. For instance, seed funds reserved for researchers trying to turn a discovery into a start-up can help nascent scholar-entrepreneurs pay for help on matters such as intellectual property rights, incorporation documents, and business plans. In this way, relatively small sums—in the tens of thousands of dollars range—can allow academics to cross the chasm from insight to commercial product.

### Appoint an Industrial Liaison Officer

Based on the importance of working with industry on cooperative terms, there exists a clear need for leaders at universities who are charged with fostering longer term relationships with the private sector and champion-ing commercialization efforts. This role, which we refer to as the indus-trial liaison officer (ILO) in keeping with language used by the ERC program, has a more strategic focus than typical university technology transfer professionals. Tech transfer officials spend much of their time executing intellectual property transactions and mediating negotiations between companies and professors. ILOs, by contrast, seek to understand private-sector needs, where scholars can take action, and what hurdles must be overcome. Successful commercialization of academic science and engineering research requires bridging between academia and industry, and ILOs act as bridges.[6] One ILO we interviewed, in noting his role as a link among industry and university researchers, stated: "Well, you people in industry, you're looking for solutions. We in academia have solutions and we're looking for problems."[7]

Our findings on the ERC program suggested that a particular approach to the ILO position is optimal. A number of ILOs saw their primary role as building industry relationships. Others acted primarily as a facilitator be-tween individual ERC researchers and the technology transfer office in an effort to make technology commercialization processes seamless for re-searchers. The ERCs with the greatest commercialization outputs, how-ever, had ILOs who blended these roles. In particular, these ILOs positioned themselves as both evangelists of the value of technology commercializa-tion and as providers of resources to researchers, the tech transfer office, and industry to coordinate effective collaboration among all participants.

### Improve Technology Transfer and Administrative Execution

We are not the first to call for more efficient and rapid technology transfer operations. But the point bears repeating. Our research found that an ef-fective technology transfer office can have a dramatic impact on commer-cialization. When a technology transfer office was perceived as having a welcoming, customer-service orientation, researchers were more likely to pursue invention disclosure and patent activities. In addition, if the office is well-organized, well-funded, and knowledgeable, it is better able to process paperwork and pursue commercialization. Unfortunately, many technology transfer offices have let their financial aspirations lead them to be hard-nosed in licensing negotiations with academic inventors and company licensees, ever trying to extract from inventors and companies contracts that have favorable financial terms for the university. Although maximizing financial gain for universities is not a bad goal in itself, the better philosophy, we believe, is to focus on speed to market. An emphasis on moving technologies to the commercial sector quickly, as MIT does, reduces friction with industry and makes it more likely that university inventions will change the world.[8]

Beyond the technology transfer office, research center staff with a process execution mindset can greatly aid technology commercialization. Given the complexity of research initiatives that may encompass dozens of scholars, several universities, and scores of industrial partners, center leaders need project management skills and competence with related software tools. The capabilities of administrative support staff should not be overlooked. We found that ERC support personnel who helped with the administrative processes required in filing an invention disclosure or patent application were highly valued assets in successful centers.

Improved execution is not about filing frivolous patent applications, giving sweetheart deals to industry, crimping academic freedom, or cutting corners on good scholarship. Indeed, the patience to engage in longer term, high-risk, high-reward projects is central to the Organized Innovation method for technology breakthroughs. Orchestrated Commercialism calls on universities to recalibrate their typical tempo in both directions— slowing down in the sense of lengthening the duration of research projects, but accelerating in the way they complete transactions such as licensing deals along the way.

### Bring in Entrepreneurial and Business Expertise

This final recommendation refers to forging formal connections to people and organizations with entrepreneurial and business knowledge and experience. Such individuals and groups encompass entrepreneurs, regional business development agencies, business education and advocacy groups, university alumni groups, local business incubators, and business schools. Ties to these people and organizations are critical because they can offer advice, support for start-ups in the form of funding or space, and a professional network that can be important for matching university technology with commercial partners.

Recall the significance of the relationship at Rice University between the Center for Biological and Environmental Nanotechnology and the Rice Alliance for Technology and Entrepreneurship in helping to launch Carbon Nanotechnologies and other start-ups. The Rice Alliance was formed as a partnership among the university's engineering school, its school of natural sciences, and its school of business. It illustrates the promise of ties between diverse schools by providing a vehicle for connecting academic researchers with entrepreneurs and early-stage investors. The Alliance did so by drawing upon the entrepreneurs, investors, and businesspeople in Rice University's alumni network, as well as those who had no affiliation with Rice. Since its inception in 2000, the Rice Alliance has assisted in the launch of more than 250 start-ups, which have raised more than $500 million in early-stage capital. The Rice Alliance also gave birth to the Rice Business Plan Competition, the largest and richest graduate student business plan competition in the world. In 2012 it awarded $1,550,000 in prize money.[9] Many universities have similar centers.[10]

Overall, university business schools are an underutilized resource in university technology commercialization. Science and engineering departments at research universities typically have limited or no relationship with business schools, which may be just a few buildings away on campus. Yet business school deans and professors can offer a wealth of experience and guidance to those inventing technology at the same institution. Also potentially valuable are business students, who can serve as employees or managers in fledgling firms, providing such help as market research, feedback on prototypes, and business plan development. Perhaps even more powerfully, business school alumni networks provide an extraordinarily rich pool of talent for start-ups.

Connectivity among business students and those in science, engineering, and medicine can be accomplished through degree courses that require interactions among the students. Non-degree short courses also can accomplish this objective. A pioneer at developing and delivering both degree and nondegree courses is Jack Gill, an engineer with a PhD in chemistry and personal connections from a forty-year career as a venture capitalist in Silicon Valley. Gill has developed such entrepreneurship courses at Harvard, MIT, Rice, Indiana, Baylor College of Medicine, and University College London. Examples of the short courses are Velocity (a joint effort of Indiana and the University of California, Berkeley) and Ignite (a joint venture of Rice, University of California, Davis, and Boston University). These courses provide both education and inspiration to students by using academics, start-up CEOs, and venture capitalists to deliver how-to education about technology entrepreneurship.

## BMES AND ORCHESTRATED COMMERCIALIZATION

The ERC program has proven to be powerful in terms of creating organizational climates that foster technology commercialization. This is largely due to the structure that ERCs require, including a formal industry liaison and a strategic plan for broader impact. Many faculty members we interviewed shared the sentiment that ERCs can and do institute broad climate change in terms of commercialization. "The ERC has helped change this culture; I now always consider [invention] disclosure issues. Before, I would not have," one faculty member told us. Another said: "I now recognize things that I'd like my research to become. This is unique from typical federal grants."

The Biomimetic MicroElectronic Systems ERC is especially emblematic of Orchestrated Commercialization. Its work to bring an artificial retina to life has begun to help an estimated 100,000 people in the United States alone who suffer from retinitis pigmentosa. The novel field of bioelectronics promises entirely new treatments for many ailments, as well as the potential for new companies and high-quality jobs.

The BMES story starts with Mark Humayun, but his isn't the mythical tale of the heroic inventor succeeding against all odds on his own. To be sure, Humayun has persevered to a degree many others would not. He has demonstrated impressive intellectual power during his quest to design a bionic eye. Yet also key to Humayun's success has been his ability to assemble an effective team—inside and outside of academia—that collectively could commercialize the artificial retina. In other words, he has coordinated the network. Humayun forged close ties early on with engineering researcher Jim Weiland and physician Eugene de Juan, Jr. at Johns Hopkins University. Together they came up with the basic concept of the artificial retina.

Step by step, the team pieced together a device they called the Argus, named after the mythical Greek giant said to have one hundred eyes and be all seeing. A digital video camera is embedded in a pair of glasses. A microprocessor worn by the patient interprets the video signal and relays it wirelessly to another set of components surgically implanted in the patient's eyeball. An array of electrodes emits pulses, which patients interpret as moving images. By 2006 Humayun's team had developed the sixty-electrode Argus II, which offers enough resolution to let patients recognize basic shapes such as people's bodies and furniture.

While they progressed on the artificial retina, Humayun and de Juan also connected with entrepreneurs—another key element of coordinating the network. Alfred Mann, an entrepreneur with a long history of successful start-ups in the technology and medical device field, cofounded Second Sight in 1998, with Sam Williams and Gunnar Bjorg. Although Humayun is not a formal cofounder of Second Sight, he worked closely with Mann, the other cofounders, and his graduate student Robert Greenberg, who became CEO of the company from the outset. Second Sight spearheaded clinical trials for the Argus in 2002 and expanded trials in 2006.

Humayun also embodied the coordinate-the-network principle by helping to recruit Italian physician Stanislao Rizzo to participate in the Argus II's trials in 2006. Rizzo is an ophthalmologist who had known Humayun for several years and was intrigued by the grand scale of his colleague's quest of artificial vision. Rizzo ultimately performed the surgery that implanted the Argus II in Riccardo Santini and several other Italian patients. As someone who has spent his life trying to help patients with eyesight problems, Rizzo speaks of the Argus II with a sense of awe. "To restore sight is a dream," he says.

Weiland says Humayun has shown an uncanny ability to connect with virtually all the "key opinion leaders" related to development of the artificial retina. Weiland, who has led the BMES thrust on the artificial retina, notes Humayun has many members in his family who have been involved in foreign service and diplomatic service. In fact, there are photos of a young Mark Humayun with his grandfather and such leading figures as China's Mao Tse Tung and India's Ghandi. A skill for building bridges is in Humayun's blood, Weiland suspects. "Mark Humayun has diplomacy—maybe in his genetics."

Humayun and his team also have sought to elevate role models. Front and center on the BMES web page is a "BMES News" section that features faculty accomplishments. The center has touted achievements such as two BMES scholars winning NSF awards for top young scientists, Weiland being quoted in a *Scientific American* story, and faculty member Ellis Meng being named a top young innovator. "We always highlighted everyone in our ERC. The students saw this first hand and hence saw the ERC faculty as role models," Humayun says.

The principle of revisiting incentive systems for researchers also applies at BMES. In recent years, the University of Southern California has changed the way it calculates faculty salaries to take into account interdisciplinary work. As we have discussed, research that crosses disciplinary boundaries makes commercialization more likely. In addition, decisions about promotion and tenure also now take into account and reward interdisciplinary scholarship. These reforms have been spearheaded by Max Nikias, USC's president. Nikias founded an ERC at USC in the 1990s, the Integrated Media Systems Center. He says his changes to USC's rewards systems stem in large part from the ERC program's requirements that scholars be given incentives to pursue interdisciplinary, commercializable projects. Nikias is grateful for the prod. "Having an ERC benefits—significantly—the rest of the university," he says. Signs that USC and

Nikias are serious about recognizing interdisciplinary work include Mark Humayun's 2012 promotion to *university professor*—a designation given to less than 1 percent of tenured professors at USC—and Jim Weiland's promotion to full professor in ophthalmology and biomedical engineering in 2013.

Another way incentives have changed at USC is through the Maseeh Entrepreneurship Prize Competition. Managed through the Viterbi School of Engineering, the competition offers $100,000 in prize money annually to engineering school faculty and students with plans to "turn seedling ideas and research into real products, companies, and solutions."[11] The competition prompted Jim Weiland, BMES Industrial Liaison Officer Jack Whalen, and Artin Petrossians, a graduate student associated with BMES, to launch a start-up company that aims to dramatically improve the lifespan of medical implants. Platinum Group Coatings (PGC) was formed in 2012 to develop technology for improving the conductivity of implant electrodes, the tiny wires that attach to nerve cells or other tissue. The researchers estimate that their technique could reduce the need for cardiac pacemaker replacement surgery, saving roughly $100,000 per patient over a twenty-five-year period.

PGC did not win the competition's $50,000 grand prize. But the start-up reflects the way BMES leaders have brought in entrepreneurial and business expertise. As part of the business plan contest, Weiland, Whalen, and Petrossians were assigned a mentor, seasoned technology industry businesswoman Karen Jaffe.

The PGC-Jaffe connection is just one of the many ways BMES has linked up with entrepreneurs. The most significant tie is the one Humayun forged with Alfred Mann. Given Mann's track record, Humayun could hardly have picked a more promising partner to commercialize the artificial retina. Companies founded by Mann include Pacesetter Systems, a heart pacemaker company currently owned by St. Jude Medical; MiniMed, an insulin pump maker now owned by Medtronic; and Advanced Bionics, which produces cochlear implants and is currently owned by Sonova. Humayun has high praise for Mann: "Mann believed and invested in the technology when everyone else though it was science fiction and too risky. He made science fiction reality by forming Second Sight and allowing us to do what we have done."

BMES also reflects another aspect of the Orchestrated Commercialization formula: appoint an industrial liaison officer. Since 2009 Jack Whalen has filled the center's ILO role. Whalen is in many ways a product of the ERC program. After earning his PhD in materials science and engineering at Johns Hopkins, he worked as a postdoctorate research fellow at BMES with Mark Humayun and Jim Weiland for about two years. Then he took a job in a start-up medical device firm. After several years in industry, Whalen returned to USC in his current post—where he works to bridge the worlds he himself has bridged. He has come to see that selecting the right scholar-participants and business partners is crucial. "A center like BMES needs academic and industrial players that are open minded and receptive to negotiating how the relationship will be formed and how discoveries will be distributed. You're taking two camps with different philosophies and asking them to come together for a mutual good."

Whalen has sought to establish long-term connections with industry partners—a sharp contrast with the transactional way many universities view technology transactional activities. "These things really boil down to the relationship. The actual, personal relationship," Whalen says. It is important to build up trust, he argues, enough for companies to be willing to share their product strategies as researchers seek possible commercialization options. "That is a very sensitive question to ask of a business. It takes a lot of trust and it takes a lot of communication."

With Whalen's help, BMES has established positive relationships with the business sector. As of early 2013 it had seventeen industry partners, including Bausch & Lomb, Medtronic, Eli Lilly, Texas Instruments, and National Semiconductor. In the last three years, the ERC has raised more than $600,000 in industry partner membership fees, and over $2 million over the entire ten-year period. It has given rise to nine start-ups, including PGC.

The progress at BMES also owes, in part, to improved technology transfer at USC—another element of the Orchestrated Commercialization formula. In 2007 the university overhauled its technology transfer office. The creation of the new Stevens Center for Innovation, a move spearheaded by then-Provost Nikias, broadened the scope of the office to include innovations beyond technology and made clear that serving the public good was paramount. Whalen credits the Stevens Center as having "a customer-service mindset." Thanks partly to the help of officials at the center, BMES has produced more than one hundred patents. Taken as a whole, BMES has achieved an impressive climate of commercialization. That climate—the way BMES has Orchestrated Commercialization—played a crucial role in the success of the artificial retina. Humayun, Weiland, and others at BMES continue to improve the device.

As dramatic as the bionic eye advances are, a still-grander vision has emerged at BMES. Humayun says medicine up to now has viewed the body as a mechanical, chemical, or genetic system. But little attention has been given to the prospects of interacting with the neuro-electrical systems pervasive to our anatomy that control our organs, memories, and moods. "Your body is a neural network," Humayun says. "What are the bioelectric signals that are going throughout it, and how do we understand them? We don't know. It's another dimension that nobody has really thought about or wanted to study. . . . You can see the iceberg below the water."

Looking back on the progress of BMES and the opportunities ahead, Weiland is bullish. He is confident he and his colleagues are on their way to launching a new technological platform and changing the practice of medicine. The artificial retina is the first step toward a host of portable microelectronic devices that communicate with nerve cells to fix or replace faulty tissue and organs. "Instead of first telling patients, 'just try a drug,' it'll be, 'first try a device,'" Weiland says.

## CHALLENGES ASSOCIATED WITH ORCHESTRATED COMMERCIALIZATION

Despite his optimism, Weiland is the first to acknowledge that the sort of commercialization-oriented scholarship he and others at BMES have pursued is not easy. He says one of the chief problems facing long-term, ambitious research projects is avoiding dead ends. "It's staying on the 'critical path,' not being diverted or distracted," he says. Picking the optimal course in research and technology development is one of several challenges to Orchestrated Commercialization that universities and researchers embracing Organized Innovation must bear in mind.

Another obstacle is the difficulty of managing all the moving pieces in Orchestrated Commercialization. Simply put, it is difficult to execute. This concern encompasses project management, but includes the need to coordinate and motivate the range of players required to move technology into the public arena. Whalen believes an ERC demands strong leadership skills. "It's got to be awarded to the right team," he says.

USC's Nikias points to a related potential pitfall. Leaders of research centers working to orchestrate commercialization must begin with a mindset that values the translation of ideas and insights into products and services that make a difference in the world. He says that of the nine ERCs that lost their funding over the years, a common thread was a leader—or principal investigator (PI)—who did not distinguish between blue-sky research and the commercialization focus required at ERCs. "They were seeing it as a traditional, big research program, not an interdisciplinary, integrated-with-industry center," he says.

Many researchers also lament their technology transfer office (TTO) as a major obstacle, one that may even discourage professors from disclosing their ideas to the TTO in the first place. Slow and bureaucratic cultures at some universities may permeate TTOs. An inefficient pace can frustrate industry partners and professors alike.

Similar to Channeled Curiosity, Orchestrated Commercialization raises concerns about research impact and integrity. Researchers and universities overly concerned with financial rewards, such as licensing fees, may prioritize research based on commercial aspirations. By seeking to make money without making a real difference, projects can end up being of modest value. Besides the possibility of skewed research aims, conflicts of interests related to commercialization can tempt scholars to manipulate or withhold research findings. Research contracts between private sector firms and universities also can lead to pressure to suppress negative findings.

These risks can be mitigated, however. Disclosure policies and research rules can prevent many if not most problems. Weiland is part of USC's ethics committee and applauds university rules that require professors to manage conflicts of interest in an appropriate manner. Among other guidelines, USC prohibits faculty with a financial interest in an experimental medical device from enrolling patients in clinical trials of the device and requires faculty to disclose such interests in presentations and publications. Also, the risk of unambitious, overly applied projects can be mitigated by careful program guidelines that demand transformative technology platform targets.

With respect to bureaucratic or ineffective TTOs, the Stevens Innovation Center and others associated with ERC programs show that a better way is possible. A recent trend in the structure of TTOs offers further hope. In some universities, TTOs are transforming into limited liability companies.[12] The advantage of the TTO as a separate company is that it is affiliated with the university without being hampered by the university's governance. Instead, it can create flexible licensing contracts and invest or hold equity in start-up companies.[13]

As for the difficulty of identifying the right leaders for, and managing the complexity of, research centers adopting Orchestrated Commercialization, BMES and other ERCs have shown it is possible to find and build effective leadership teams. Center leaders may not be able to completely prevent researchers from going down dead ends, but the ERC program offers guidance on limiting such unproductive forays. In particular, NSF's frequent feedback to ERCs and the required use of strategic planning help centers stay on track. In this way, the centers tend to invest resources in the highest-potential projects that support their mission and strategic plan.

## MOON SIGHTINGS AND MOON SHOTS

Riccardo Santini may be glad to see the light of day again, but one of his high points with the artificial retina took place at night. He wanted another glimpse of a celestial body that has forever captured our imagination. "I was looking for the moon," he says. "And I saw something." Santini isn't 100 percent sure he saw the moon. But perhaps with the next generation of the Argus he will see it with certainty. Mark Humayun, his team, and the broader innovation ecosphere that includes Second Sight continue to make progress.

It is fitting, in fact, that Santini spoke of seeing the moon with his artificial retina. A BMES industrial advisory board member told Weiland that the device was akin to the NASA moon shot. That decade-long quest to send a man to the moon was one of the greatest technological achievements in human history. Restoring sight to those who are blind surely belongs in the same category. We need more moon shots, more daring— but doable—attempts to solve big problems with scientific and engineering advances.

We have developed a framework, Organized Innovation, to realistically shoot for the moon in field after field. Now we need the will to put it in place. Next we turn to our prescriptions for what government, businesses, and universities ought to do to make Organized Innovation a reality.

### NOTES

1. Committee on Research Universities et al., *Research Universities and the Future of America*, 7.
2. President's Council of Advisors on Science and Technology (PCAST), *Transformation and Opportunity*, 1.
3. Ibid., 6.
4. Dyer, Gregersen, and Christensen, *Innovator's DNA*; Hargadon, *How Breakthroughs Happen*.
5. Bercovitz and Feldman, "Academic Entrepreneurs." The authors found that working among colleagues and a department chair who are successful at commercialization increases the likelihood an individual will commercialize.
6. O'Shea, Chugh, and Allen, "Determinants and Consequences"; Roberts, *Entrepreneurs in High Technology*; Thursby and Thursby, "Are Faculty Critical?"
7. Hunter, Perry, and Currall, "Inside Multi-Disciplinary Science and Engineering Research Centers."
8. Bowen et al., "Langer Lab."
9. Rice University Business Plan Competition, "$1.55 Million in Prizes."
10. Examples of some of the most well-known university entrepreneurship centers are the Blank Center at Babson College; Entrepreneurship@Cornell;

Institute for Leadership and Entrepreneurship at Georgia Tech; Johnson Center at Indiana University; Deshpande Center at MIT; Stanford Technology Ventures Program; Lester Center at University of California, Berkeley; Child Family Institute for Innovation and Entrepreneurship at the University of California, Davis; Price Center at the University of California, Los Angeles; von Liebig Center at the University of California, San Diego; Zell-Lurie Institute at the University of Michigan; Center for Entrepreneurial Studies at the University of North Carolina, Chapel Hill; Kelleher Center at University of Texas, Austin; Batten Institute at the University of Virginia; and Burek Center at the University of Washington.

11. Maseeh Entrepreneurship Prize Competition, "About the Prize."

12. In 2009, ten of eighty-one TTOs surveyed were set up as separate incorporated companies, and the number is likely growing. Take, for instance, Imperial Innovations, a TTO that was founded for Imperial College London and now collaborates with three other major universities: Cambridge, Oxford, and University College London. Imperial Innovations registered with the London Stock Exchange in 2006 and has since raised more than £200 million and invested £121 million in a diverse portfolio of companies. See Association of University Technology Managers, *Transaction Survey*, 7, and Imperial Innovations, "About Imperial Innovations."

13. Wood, "Improving Governance Arrangements."

PART THREE

*The Prescription*

# CHAPTER 8

# Organizing Our Innovation Ecosystem

By now, we hope we have convinced you that Organized Innovation is a vital way forward as America seeks to generate societal benefits through technology breakthroughs. We have analyzed the problem: the country's R&D gap and unorganized approach to technology development, rooted in three myths about innovation. We have explained our framework as a solution, one inspired by the successful ERC program. And we have described each of the three pillars—Channeled Curiosity, Boundary-Breaking Collaboration, and Orchestrated Commercialization—that make up Organized Innovation.

So what will it take to put the Organized Innovation framework in place? What are the tangible steps our country must take, the concrete policies we ought to adopt to move forward from unorganized innovation to an organized innovation ecosystem that strengthens US leadership in the global economic landscape? In this chapter, we spell out our prescriptions for what the three main institutions in the framework—universities, businesses, and government—can do to improve America's innovation efforts.

A few features of our recommendations stand out. Universities can use the framework to turn current challenges into opportunities to revitalize their central role in America's well-being. Businesses with a longer term perspective can tap Organized Innovation to become more innovative themselves, and to capitalize on more fruitful relationships with universities. For government, the benefits of Organized Innovation can begin without costing the country a dime more than it already spends on research investments. What is more, the policies we are calling for produce potential common ground for liberals and conservatives, Democrats and Republicans. In short, what we propose is a Bipartisan Plan for government, a Wise Bet for businesses, and a Grand Bargain for universities.

## A BIPARTISAN PLAN FOR MAXIMIZING RETURN ON INVESTMENT IN RESEARCH FUNDING

We believe that US policymakers and legislators should place greater emphasis on research funding programs that embody Organized Innovation principles to harvest a better return on government research investments. We are not against a larger federal R&D budget. In fact, we agree with the recommendations made by the *Gathering Storm* report authors, who called for doubling the federal research budget over the course of seven years.[1] But increasing the federal research budget is best seen as a necessary yet not sufficient condition for improving our nation's innovation ecosystem. Simply allocating more money is not enough. We also must optimize research investments.

Our plan to increase the return on investment (ROI) of government spending on research involves steering more of our federal research dollars toward projects that incorporate Organized Innovation principles. We believe that a larger share of government research spending channeled toward practical, commercial results will lead to new technology platforms, companies, and industries. To that end, the National Science Foundation, National Institutes of Health, Department of Energy, and other agencies should fund more proposals that reflect the tenets of Organized Innovation. We should require grant applicants to plan their commercialization strategies just as carefully as they map out their basic research agenda.

How would academic science, engineering, and medical researchers do so when they have had little experience with commercialization? The answer lies partly in urging them to forge relationships with scholars from multiple disciplines, industry partners, and business school faculty colleagues. If an Organized Innovation emphasis is required for federal grants, researchers will be more motivated to seek out those relationships that, in turn, help to sustain their research programs and maximize their societal impact. The more researchers can aim for practical and commercializable outcomes, the greater the payoffs we will see from our government research investments.

We imagine some exceptions. Fields such as astronomy, theoretical physics, and theoretical mathematics may have only very distant connections, if any, to practical applications. The new knowledge such fields create is good simply for its own sake. And we are not saying that blue-sky, basic research funding should be withdrawn in those and other fields. Even some of the most prominent professors who embody the principles of Organized Innovation remain staunch advocates of curiosity-driven, basic science. These individuals include Robert Langer and Doug Lauffenburger of MIT. Lauffenburger makes the point that you can never tell when curiosity-driven, basic research will be critical in the future. "We need all types" of research, Lauffenburger says. "So much of what ends up being useful, you don't know at the time." We respect such views. We know blue-sky, basic research is valuable and can have important effects.

What is the ideal proportion of government-funded research that is purely curiosity-driven science versus research funding with more real-world potential based on Organized Innovation? The answer is unclear. That is primarily because we do not know how much Organized Innovation oriented research is under way at the moment. The current figures provided by the National Science Foundation for "basic research," "applied research," and "development" do not capture whether the science in question combines the three crucial elements, namely, an orientation toward tangible problems and solutions, the facilitation of collaboration, and co-ordination toward commercialization. Current measurements, in other words, fail to capture the amount of federal research spending that has realistic potential for technology breakthroughs. We therefore also recommend that the federal government—most likely, the National Science Foundation—measure federally funded research that is consistent with the principles of Organized Innovation on an annual basis. We imagine an assessment could be developed that measures current research projects on the extent to which they demonstrate the behaviors and activities of Channeled Curiosity, Boundary-Breaking Collaboration, and Orchestrated Commercialization. The overall evaluation of federally funded Organized Innovation should specify the amount of such research in absolute dollar terms and as a percentage of total federal research spending. Once we have those tallies, a meaningful discussion of the proper amount of Organized Innovation-oriented research can follow.

In addition to using Organized Innovation principles as criteria for awarding research grants, such grants should be assessed periodically using the Organized Innovation framework. Building on the tradition of the ERC program, federal grants awarded using the Organized Innovation criteria should have to demonstrate every few years that they are living up to the principles of Channeled Curiosity, Boundary-Breaking Collaboration, and Orchestrated Commercialization. Such monitoring must be balanced against the need to keep paperwork and reporting expectations modest. As well, we believe a "coaching to improve" approach to research centers on the part of supervising federal agencies—as opposed to a strictly evaluative stance—should be part of all Organized Innovation efforts. On the other hand, we agree with the way NSF officials in charge of the ERC program have terminated funding for underperforming ERCs.[2] Government-sponsored research that intends to fulfill Organized Innovation principles yet fails to do so on an ongoing basis should lose funding.

Besides orienting research more toward Organized Innovation principles, the country ought to measure the return on investment in such projects. Doing so is not simple, however. Assessing job creation stemming from research investments is one crucial economic outcome; others include the improved quality of the workforce, savings to businesses, and new revenue brought into the economy by the activities surrounding Organized Innovation projects.[3] Upstream from such quantifiable economic impacts are a variety of technology transfer metrics, such as patent awards, licenses, start-up companies, and the number and commercial growth of companies located in university-led research parks or incubators. But these traditional technology transfer metrics may tend to severely underestimate the quantitative economic return of centers such as ERCs.[4] A further complication is the timing of assessments. If measured too early, impact may not yet be realized. If measured too late, records may be more difficult to access and sources of impact may be more diffuse. Also if we rely too much on quantitative outcomes, we may miss intangible impacts.

Those intangibles often go by the name of *knowledge transfer*, which refers to any and all flow of new information from the scholarly community to society.[5] It may be distinguished from the conventional definitions of technology transfer in that knowledge transfer emphasizes that there are many ways scholarly work moves into society that do not involve tangible technology or intellectual property.[6] The concept of knowledge transfer is important for another reason: it encompasses the indispensible value to society of research in social sciences and the humanities, as well as creative works developed by visual and performing artists. In fact, social sciences, humanities, and the arts can provide insights into how and why the public embraces or rejects new technological innovations. Without such understanding, many brilliant technologies will fall short of their potential societal impact.[7] Any full assessment of ROI of Organized Innovation must include various forms of knowledge transfer to capture the range of broad and long-term impacts. (See Appendix A for more on how ROI has been assessed for the ERC program.)

Our call for orienting federal research funding decisions toward the Organized Innovation framework is complementary to some proposals currently circulating among government leaders for increasing the return on federal research investments. One reform idea is to bolster programs that have focused on translating research into commercial results, such as the US Commerce Department's i6 Challenge. The i6 Challenge seeks to accelerate innovative product development, spur the formation of start-ups, and create small businesses by supporting proof of concept centers at universities and research consortiums.[8] Proof of concept centers carry out activities as we discussed in chapter 4, and they supply evidence to existing companies or potential entrepreneurs that an innovation is ready (or not) to be developed into a marketable product.

NSF in recent years also has taken actions that are akin to the ideas we have proposed with Organized Innovation. Subra Suresh, who headed NSF from 2010 to 2013, started two progressive programs to generate innovative collaborations and cultivate the commercial implications of NSF-funded research. To foster research that breaks down academic silos, Suresh launched an initiative called Integrated NSF Support Promoting Interdisciplinary Research and Education (INSPIRE). Suresh also launched the NSF Innovation Corps (I-Corps), which prepares scientists and engineers to broaden the impact of NSF-funded, basic-research projects. In commenting on I-Corps, Suresh stated, "a lot of the projects we fund don't go beyond a publication. That's not because the PIs [principal investigators] aren't capable of taking it further, but because some don't have the opportunity to do it at the institutions in which they work." I-Corps is intended to provide that opportunity.[9]

Making Organized Innovation one criterion for federal R&D funding would serve as an umbrella policy for the i6 Challenge, I-Corps, and other initiatives to commercialize more research. It goes beyond incremental steps to offer a deeper reform of the existing US system of science funding. It acknowledges that years of asking researchers to consider and name the "broader impacts" of their research have not produced enough success.

In fact, Organized Innovation as one basis for federal research funding decisions could go a long way toward improving the rate of commercialization of government grants. Currently, the rate is roughly 2 percent, according to Nish Acharya, the former director of the Office of Innovation and Entrepreneurship in the US Department of Commerce's Economic Development Administration.[10] Acharya argues that the country should aim to hit a commercialization rate of 5 percent by 2020. We agree. We also agree with Acharya's observation that focusing much more attention on commercialization in federal research will require significant training in the ranks of officials at agencies such as NSF, NIH, DOE, and the Department of Commerce. Some of those government officials who shape research programs, award grants, and monitor progress have facility with moving basic research to the realm of the market. But they are the exception rather than the rule, Acharya says. Also crucial to this government upskilling will be selecting agency leaders comfortable with the specific tasks involved in commercialization of research.

Adopting Organized Innovation as a guiding principle of government funding will likely ruffle some feathers in government. It might be poorly received by government agency officials who swear by "pure" scientific research. Organized Innovation also might be viewed skeptically by those on either extreme side of the political spectrum—by conservatives wary of any government intervention in the economy and by liberals suspicious of involving industry in academic science. In the wake of increasing stalemates in Washington and a stubbornly tepid recovery, many Americans overall doubt government can effectively address social and economic dilemmas.

But we think the time is right to remind citizens, elected officials, and public servants that America has a rich tradition of rolling up its sleeves to coordinate large-scale technology solutions to tough challenges. We face one now. As we argued in chapter 2, the country's drift toward unorganized innovation has eroded America's competitiveness in the global economy. Our nation's prosperity—and to a large extent the world's well-being—are at stake. But the United States has succeeded in the past in launching big projects when the stakes were high. Examples include the Manhattan Project to build an atomic bomb during World War II, the Tennessee Valley Authority to modernize much of Appalachia, and the Apollo moon shots—which were undertaken, in part, to demonstrate our ability to compete in the Cold War space race.

The Internet is yet another example of a publicly guided technology project that dramatically changed our economy and society—for the better, most would agree. And it is one with direct relevance to the principles of Organized Innovation because its origins are in a government–university partnership. Neal Lane, former director of the White House Office of Science and Technology Policy and former director of the National Science Foundation, notes that the Internet's roots lie in a network of university supercomputing centers funded by NSF. The Advanced Research Projects Agency (ARPA, later to become the Defense Advanced Research Projects Agency, DARPA) developed a network of computers, and NSF subsequently used ARPANET as the backbone to create the computer network serving the NSF-funded supercomputer centers. Later, the network came to be used by members of the public and companies. Commercial Internet service providers began to emerge in the late 1980s and early 1990s.[11] It is hard to argue that the government erred by investing in the novel networking technologies, with roots in universities, that eventually became today's Internet. It amounted to a bet on a platform that spawned a commercial boom, a bet that paid off for the country and its citizens, as well as for the entire world. We are confident examples like this can overcome public pessimism about large-scale cooperation and coordination among government, academia, and industry.

We also believe the Organized Innovation framework should appeal to politicians of the two major parties and to citizens overall, regardless of political leanings. Republicans and conservatives can appreciate the way the framework emphasizes a large role for entrepreneurship and free enterprise, tapping industry's expertise and ability to bring new technologies to scale. Democrats and liberals should find it appealing that government, acting as a force for collective good, plays a more significant role in economic growth by strategically harmonizing the national innovation ecosystem. Organized Innovation, in other words, has a real chance to come to fruition despite today's polarized political climate. It is fundamentally a bipartisan plan.

## A WISE BET FOR BUSINESSES

Organized Innovation also merits support from the business community. Already, industry is largely behind calls for greater R&D funding with a commercialization bent.[12] But Organized Innovation is not a free lunch for companies, nor can the country afford for its industrial sector to passively await the results of more practical-minded university research. For businesses to truly reap the benefits of Organized Innovation efforts—and for the efforts to have the optimal effect on America as a whole—companies must fully buy into the approach.

In part, that means contributing financially to university research centers. ERCs, for example, work with many industrial partners who contribute dollar amounts ranging from a thousand dollars to tens of thousands or more. Some of these companies pay membership fees, which help pay for important equipment, for the stipends of graduate students and postdoctoral fellows, and for other overhead costs needed to coordinate the centers effectively. In addition, companies ought to consider directly sponsoring more research and development projects at universities. At ERCs, such projects are explicitly encouraged. They often take the form of more-applied, commercial prototype development.

Business investment in university-based research centers must go beyond the financial, however. For Organized Innovation to truly succeed, companies must commit to long-term partnerships with universities and scholars. They must assign representatives to advise their academic partners regarding possible market demand for new technology platforms or products based on university research, to sit through detailed discussions of project challenges and offer guidance, and to devote time to periodic strategy meetings of center officials. This means a business investment in the knowledge and social capital of their employees and a willingness to work with scholars, who may sometimes frustrate industry with the way they prize knowledge dissemination over intellectual property protection. In other words, businesses have to move away from concentrating narrowly on short-term gains through incremental product advances to put serious effort and energy into bigger picture technology platforms.

The potential payoff is big—both for society and for private sector companies. When industry plays an active role in helping academics to pick meaningful problems, guiding those research efforts in productive directions, and moving the resulting discoveries toward commercialization, America as a whole benefits through a better return on its technology investments. Individual businesses also stand to reap strong gains from involving themselves in Organized Innovation efforts. For example, joining forces with university-based research centers can allow companies to share and lower their innovation-related risks. That is, rather than spend millions on a traditional industrial lab with fixed costs, companies can effectively outsource some of the work to scholars. This is increasingly an appealing strategy as technology development becomes more global in scale and advances can come rapidly from a variety of sources, including individuals, government labs, companies, and universities.

Even as businesses share risks in Organized Innovation efforts, they also share in the rewards. These rewards can include early access to intellectual property. University research centers, for example, can specify a master intellectual property template agreement for licensing contracts to companies that have a formal affiliation with the center. Also, industry partner firms may be given the opportunity to license the intellectual property before it is offered to nonpartner firms. Direct industry sponsorship of research also can lead to tangible products.

What is more, companies profit from access to students who can become future employees. Brad Bohlmann, of the Center for Compact and Efficient Fluid Power, said his center's industry partners prize above all else their access to students—working with them and considering them as potential employees. "We went in naively thinking that the intellectual property the center creates was going to be the primary goal of our industry members. They've told us that IP is great, but it's icing on the cake. The cake is made of students," Bohlmann says.

Companies can also profit from the broader expertise that comes from connections with scholars and the broader community that develops at collaborative research centers. Consider the approach Intel takes. It has established seven Intel Science and Technology Centers in the United States and five Intel Collaborative Research Institutes in Europe and Asia. Each aims to create a multidisciplinary community of researchers. "We look to these centers and institutes for the long-range research work that was typical of that being done at Bell Labs in the '40s and '50s and Xerox PARC in the '70s and '80s," says Justin Rattner, director of Intel Labs.[13] In other words, for Intel and other companies, Organized Innovation represents a wise bet.

## A GRAND BARGAIN FOR UNIVERSITIES

If Organized Innovation represents common ground for politicians and a wise bet for businesses, it offers a grand bargain for American universities. For public universities, the framework provides a way to address today's twin crises of funding and reputation. In part because of the recent recession and tepid recovery, public universities have experienced major budget cuts. Consider the University of California (UC), often regarded as the preeminent state university system in the country, if not the world. For the year 2011–12, UC's state-funded undesignated support was $2.37 billion, a 21.3 percent drop from the previous year. That dramatic decrease comes on top of years of smaller hits: the state's per-student funding for UC education has fallen roughly 60 percent since 1990.[14] The University of California and other universities have been forced to respond to the cuts in part by raising tuition. Private colleges also have hiked fees at a fast clip. Between 2000 and 2011, prices for undergraduate tuition, room, and board at public institutions rose 42 percent, and prices at private, not-for-profit institutions rose 31 percent, after adjustment for inflation.[15]

There are some legitimate reasons for those increases. But the soaring costs of college have left a sour taste in the public's mouth. A 2011 Pew Research Center report found that 57 percent of Americans say the higher education system in the United States fails to provide students with good value for the money they and their families spend.[16] Most American parents still expect their children to attend college, but there are signs of deep disenchantment with US universities.

Against this backdrop, Organized Innovation offers the prospect of a new compact between universities and the society they serve. Leading the charge toward new technology platforms would elevate universities in the public's eye. Skepticism about higher education could well transform into an appreciation of the promise of basic research and the importance of academia. Students will also be served by increased opportunities to engage in real-world research. Channeled Curiosity can help students see the broader potential of basic research. Boundary-Breaking Collaboration allows students to initiate relationships with companies that can lead to future job options. Orchestrated Commercialization can offer real entrepreneurial opportunities for students as they enter the workforce. Organized Innovation, in other words, provides universities with an opportunity to improve their public standing even as they provide students with an improved educational experience.

But to enjoy these benefits, universities will have to redouble their commitments to society. As with businesses and government, universities must change their business as usual. In the previous chapters, we have provided details of the steps academic institutions ought to take to accomplish Organized Innovation.[17] They must orient scientific research toward real-world goals (Channeled Curiosity), facilitate collaboration of a diverse nature (Boundary-Breaking Collaboration), and coordinate the commercialization of novel technology (Orchestrated Commercialization). These three pillars ultimately boil down to a simple but challenging prescription: universities must engage more with society. They must envision meaningful problems to tackle. They must work more cooperatively with industry. They must roll up their sleeves and work hard to transfer their nascent technologies into the public and commercial spheres.

One institution poised to demonstrate the benefits of university engagement is the Francis Crick Institute in London. The still-under-development biomedical institute is a partnership of University College London, Imperial College London, and King's College London, as well as the Wellcome Trust Sanger Institute, and its leaders are determined to steer research in practical yet innovative directions. Crick executives Nurse, Treisman, and Smith talk about:

> a place where laboratory biologists are encouraged to collaborate with clinical researchers to understand the medical implications of their work, with pharmaceutical companies for the translation of discoveries into treatments, and with physical scientists to expand their thinking and repertoire of experimental approaches. Such an institution must be continually open to new ideas and permeable to interactions with outside researchers and organizations.[18]

This example is illustrative of a broader trend. To some extent in recent decades, the pendulum has swung away from the isolated, esoteric extreme of the ivory tower. But universities must move further toward a sense of responsibility for the economic and social well-being of the country and the globe. At the same time, they must do so without going so far in the direction of commercial concerns that they lose their soul. Universities must not allow industry to dictate research priorities or squelch academic freedom or ignore pressing public problems while seeking to make a fast buck on a trivial technology.

We are convinced that American universities can strike this balance. For guidance, they can take a page from their history. US land grant colleges were launched in 1862 by President Abraham Lincoln with a mission tied to economic progress. In particular, the central purpose of the land grant institutions was

> without excluding other scientific and classical studies and including military tactic, to teach such branches of learning as are related to agriculture and the mechanic arts, in such manner as the legislatures of the States may respectively prescribe, in order to promote the liberal and practical education of the industrial classes in the several pursuits and professions in life.[19]

The notion of a grand bargain was embedded in the very origins of these institutions. The Morrill Acts of 1862 and 1890 granted federal government land to states in exchange for their promise to establish practical-minded colleges. Ultimately, the land grant colleges proved to play a major role in the country's economic and social development in the nineteenth and twentieth centuries.[20]

An emphasis on public engagement, though, has gotten lost at some land grant universities over the years. It is missing at many other American universities as well. Linda Katehi, chancellor of the University of California, Davis, notes that scholars in her field of engineering are well equipped to solve a "problem." But much of the time they pick a problem in a vacuum, without the insight or input of industry partners. And, therefore, they pick one of very limited significance. "They are not necessarily defining the problem well," she says. As chancellor of a land grant university, Katehi has aimed to improve engagement efforts through steps such as streamlining the licensing process and teaching commercialization skills to faculty. As she sees it, many university officials mistakenly view academic freedom and economic development as conflicting rather than complementary goals. What is needed, she says, is a rethinking of the very mission of public universities. "Universities need to do a better job of revising the ideal of the land grant college, and create a new interpretation that will make it more current and contemporary."

For guidance in that effort, a number of universities stand out as role models. For example, MIT's approach to licensing deals with industry favors speed over lucrative terms. MIT may lose about 10 percent in revenue by trying to strike licensing deals quickly rather than bargaining extensively for better terms—but quick deals fit the university's mission of disseminating knowledge.[21] Stanford, whose engaged culture gave birth to Silicon Valley, has taken the lead in tearing down boundaries. Consider Stanford's Mayfield Fellows Program. It is a nine-month work-study program provided to a dozen students annually that combines the study of entrepreneurship, innovation, and leadership with a summer job at a Silicon Valley start-up. Another university embracing innovation on campus is the University of North Carolina, Chapel Hill. In 2010, then-chancellor Holden Thorp launched the Office of Innovation and Entrepreneurship, which aims to help faculty, students, and staff "translate their novel ideas into practical benefit and change the world." The initiative includes a Faculty Bootcamp that encourages an entrepreneurial mindset and the Carolina Express License, which echoes MIT's emphasis on speedy deals.[22] The University of Southern California also has become a leader in technology transfer and innovation in recent years, thanks partly to President Max Nikias. As mentioned earlier, Nikias spearheaded the creation of an ERC in 1996 while a professor in the school's engineering department. He credits the program for shifting his thinking toward a greater engagement with real-world problems as well as increased facility with setting a vision, planning a strategy, and delivering results. "I consider myself a product of the ERC program," he says, and he argues professors must become more active in working to solve societal problems. "Most of them have to come down from the ivory tower and go into the town square."

This greater societal commitment of those universities, and many others, is important for deepening bonds with companies, foundations, and philanthropic donors. In fact, a new reciprocal compact between higher education and society can strengthen the financial foundations of public and private universities in the form of philanthropic income. Many university leaders believe that deeper connections with a range of stakeholders are the gateway for future philanthropic gifts, which in the long run may have a larger financial impact than sponsored research or intellectual property. Philanthropic revenues are particularly flexible in that they can be used either for the endowment or current use expenditures, such as new facility construction. Clearly, an enlightened relationship strategy is paying off for many universities with respect to philanthropic giving. Anecdotally, consider the gifts raised in 2012 by the sample of universities mentioned above: MIT: $379,058,315; Stanford: $1,034,848,797; North Carolina: $286,709,822; and USC: $491,853,719. Stanford set a record by being the first university to raise over $1 billion in a single year.[23]

## Engaging Academics

Our call for universities to change, to accept a new grand bargain is already welcomed by many university administrators. The tougher crowd to convince may be the faculty. It may be that winning over scholars—in science, engineering, and medicine as well as those in the humanities, social sciences, and professional schools—will be the most challenging obstacle to Organized Innovation succeeding in America. It will be vital to convince faculty members to adopt a more expansive view of the role of research and scholarship, and to channel their curiosity toward societal benefit.

To help speed the transition, we reiterate our call for reforms to the incentive systems for faculty and the criteria for promotion and tenure. To be sure, faculty at all ranks need to establish and maintain credibility within their own discipline.[24] But scholars should be rewarded as well for interdisciplinary, collaborative efforts to transfer knowledge and for commercialization of novel technologies. Encouragingly, there is a move toward a broader conceptualization of research and scholarly "impact."

One example of this broader view of research and scholarly impact is the recent change to faculty promotion and tenure guidelines at the University of Arizona. In her inaugural address as the new president of the university, Ann Weaver Hart stated: "We will need to create new knowledge with new partners and in new places for us to be able to achieve the vision of the 21st century land-grant university."[25] Subsequently, the Faculty Senate approved a proposal to reshape the promotion and tenure guidelines with the following emphasis:

> The University values an inclusive view of scholarship in the recognition that knowledge is acquired and advanced through discovery, integration, application and teaching. Given this perspective, promotion and tenure reviews, as detailed in the criteria of individual departments and colleges, will recognize original research contributions in peer-reviewed publications as well as integrative and applied forms of scholarship that involve cross-cutting collaborations with business and community partners, including translational research, commercialization activities and patents.[26]

Despite these new trends in faculty performance evaluation, commercially oriented research remains unfamiliar to many faculty members and is often looked down upon. Just ask Kyriacos Athanasiou, professor of biomedical engineering and orthopedic surgery at the University of California, Davis. Athanasiou has been pursuing practical solutions based on his research for decades. Among his start-up companies is Vidacare, whose drill-like technology delivers drugs rapidly into bone tissue—which can be vital to treating patients in crises such as cardiac arrest. But Athanasiou says entrepreneurial achievements and activities in academia often are viewed with suspicion in what he calls a "climate of negativity."

At the same time, Athanasiou sees that climate changing. More and more scholars, he says, are interested in making a difference beyond the confines of academia. We are hopeful this trend will continue—that academics will recognize the ways greater engagement and the principles of Organized Innovation can make their careers even more meaningful than blue-sky research alone. Athanasiou, for example, once received a note from the wife of someone who benefited from one of his products. Her husband was a fireman in his early fifties who collapsed, went into shock, and was close to death. But an emergency medical technician used Vidicare technology to revive him. The wife thanked Athanasiou "from the bottom of my heart." The note warmed Athanasiou's heart and further fueled his approach to scholarship. As he puts it, "I don't think there's anything more exciting than coming up with an idea, and then years later, seeing the idea become a product helping people."

## NOTES

1. National Academies, *Rising above the Gathering Storm: Energizing and Employing: Energizing and Employing America for a Brighter Future.*
2. Lynn Preston, leader of the ERC program, interview with the authors, April 3, 2013.
3. Roessner, Manrique, and Park, "Economic Impact of Engineering Research Centers."
4. Ibid.
5. Malakoff, "Making Academic Research Pay Off."
6. Knowledge transfer also includes when researchers publish in journals or books that are read by R&D managers or business executives in the field. Executives and managers might also attend workshops held by academics, or professors might provide consulting services.
7. Currall et al., "What Drives Public Acceptance?"
8. US Department of Commerce, "Acting Secretary Blank Announces."
9. Mervis, "Suresh Leaves His Mark."

10. Acharya says the 2 percent figure is not based on a formal study but is an estimate widely accepted among federal officials.
11. *Wikipedia*, "National Science Foundation Network" and "Internet."
12. Augustine, "America's Competitiveness."
13. Henneman, "Not Your Grandfather's Industrial Lab."
14. UC Office of the President, "UC Budget."
15. US Department of Education, National Center for Education Statistics, "Fast Facts."
16. Taylor et al., *Is College Worth It?*
17. Currall, "Stewarding the University of California Dream."
18. Nurse, Treisman, and Smith, "Building Better Institutions."
19. Our Documents, "Transcript of Morrill Act."
20. Fogel and Malson-Huddle, *Precipice or Crossroads?*
21. Bowen et al., "Langer Lab."
22. Cone, Progress Report Year Two.
23. Chronicle of Higher Education, *Almanac 2013–2014*, 57.
24. Given most current promotion and tenure systems, we caution against junior faculty researchers focusing too broadly outside their discipline. That means that individuals must make careful decisions about what type of research is appropriate within their institution.
25. University of Arizona, Office of University Communications, "UA Adds Tech Transfer."
26. Ibid.

# CHAPTER 9

# Seeing Is Believing

Americans are gloomy about their future. Amid a lackluster economic recovery, woes about the national debt, and technological advances abroad, many fear our best days as a technology and economic leader may be behind us.

Our problems are real. But perhaps our biggest problem has to do with our vision. It has diminished; we have lost our ability to discern the roots of our troubles. An innovation gap, where US universities often focus on esoteric basic research and industry concentrates on incremental product development, has widened in recent decades. And the country has failed to close the gap in large part because of myths about lone geniuses, about the free market, and about innovation itself. These myths have obscured our sense of what's wrong and how to fix it.

Yet there is a long human tradition of regaining sight, of the scales falling from our eyes. This is one of those moments. It's time for America to open its eyes and see its innovation challenge for what it truly is—a dysfunctional system of unorganized innovation. It is time to embrace a new solution, by organizing innovation effectively. Based on nearly a decade of rigorous quantitative and qualitative research, we have developed the Organized Innovation framework as a prescription for how our nation can move forward. Organized Innovation addresses the innovation gap before us; corresponds to the collaborative, brokered way innovation happens best; and can be put into practice today to the benefit of both our country and the world.

At a national level, our blueprint for a more organized innovation ecosystem can produce better returns on our federal investments, as we discussed in the previous chapter. At the level of universities, it means leaders must implement the three pillars of the Organized Innovation framework as they envision and structure their research programs. To recap the key points of the framework, Organized Innovation means:

(1) Channeled Curiosity—Orienting basic research questions toward practical ends that have great social and economic potential. It can be accomplished through five actions:

- Lead with vision
- Pursue technology platforms
- Plan strategically
- Synthesize solutions
- Persist with the process

(2) Boundary-Breaking Collaboration—Facilitating cooperation among researchers of different disciplines and institutions, and between academics and the private sector, for more effective, relevant results. It can be accomplished through six actions:

- Lead through persuasion and trust
- Create interdependence
- Promote collaboration across academic disciplines
- Connect with industry
- Link universities
- Seek active dialogue with government representatives

(3) Orchestrated Commercialization—Coordinating efforts of researchers, university administrators, industry partners, and others to develop new technologies and bring them out of academia and into the public sphere. It can be accomplished through six actions:

- Coordinate the network
- Elevate role models
- Revisit incentives for commercializing academic research
- Appoint an industrial liaison officer
- Improve technology transfer and administrative execution
- Bring in entrepreneurial and business expertise

Our framework represents a call to action for the three key institutions in Organized Innovation: universities, businesses, and government. As we have discussed, there are powerful reasons for all the players to welcome Organized Innovation. Universities find themselves amid reduced funding, significant public skepticism regarding their value, and scholarship that is often decoupled from societal needs. Companies with operations in the United States find themselves with limited research budgets and struggling to stay abreast of technological advances occurring around the globe. And the US government—indeed its entire citizenry—faces unprecedented competition in technological and economic realms; a possible decline in its standard of living; and complex, weighty problems such as climate change, international terrorism, and the emergence of new deadly diseases.

All these institutions are poised to shed their innovation-blinders. Showing them how to do so is the story of the ERC program. Its quarter century of success helps belie the myths that have constrained our innovation ecosystem. As we have explained, ERCs have spawned inspiring new technology platforms: a novel hydraulic system proven to slash fuel emissions in construction equipment; protein therapies and tissue engineering methods that are improving lives or promising to do so; the artificial retina that is restoring sight to the blind.

The success of Mark Humayun and the innovation hotbed he has created at the Biomimetic Electronic Systems ERC can be measured in part by numbers of patent filings, by start-up funding raised, by commercial sales, and by jobs created. But perhaps the best signs come in the form of moments like those experienced by Filippo Tenaglia. Like Riccardo Santini, Tenaglia was among the first patients to receive the Argus II artificial retina. At age twenty-six, he lost his sight to retinitis pigmentosa and was forced to use "the white cane." After five years of blindness, the bionic eye entered his life, and brightened it considerably.

Tenaglia wondered if this new digital form of sight would allow him to gaze into the eyes of someone. So he focused on the face of his girlfriend. "I was trying to look at her eyes, and a pixel lights up. I realized it was probably the reflection of light in her eyes," he recalls. "I realized it was possible."

This is the sort of modern-day miracle of which we are capable—technology breakthroughs that not only create jobs and promote prosperity but that lift the human spirit. For too long, our approach to technology innovation has been disorganized, and as a result, disheartening. Let's enter a new era, refocus our vision, and regain our faith. Let's organize innovation for a more prosperous future.

# ACKNOWLEDGMENTS

Some of the material in this book is based upon work supported by the National Science Foundation (NSF) under Grant No. EEC-0345195. Any opinions, findings, conclusions, or recommendations expressed in this book are those of the authors and survey respondents or interviewees, and do not necessarily reflect the official views, opinions, or policy of the NSF.

We thank Lynn Preston and Linda Parker of the NSF for support and guidance of this research. In conducting our research, we benefited greatly from the counsel of the members of our NSF grant's Technical Advisory Board, each of whom was a sitting director of an Engineering Research Center (ERC): Brij M. Moudgil, University of Florida; Robert M. Nerem, Georgia Institute of Technology; Buddy D. Ratner, University of Washington; Farhang Shadman, University of Arizona; and Michael B. Silevitch, Northeastern University. Vicki L. Colvin, Rice University, also was a member of the board (although her center was a Nanoscale Science and Engineering Center). Courtland Lewis of SciTech Communications gave valuable input throughout the research and writing of this book as well. We also thank Mary Sommers Pyne and Timmie Wang at the Rice Alliance for Technology and Entrepreneurship at Rice University, and Sally and Cimon Chee of Rice University for their assistance.

In addition, we thank all the people we interviewed for this book, including Mark S. Humayun, James D. Weiland, and J. Jack Whalen at the Biomimetic MicroElectronic Systems ERC; Kim A. Stelson, Brad Bohlmann, James Van de Ven, Zongxuan "Sunny" Sun, and Duane "Dewey" Tinderholm at the Center for Compact and Efficient Fluid Power; Harvey F. Lodish, Robert S. Langer, Douglas S. Lauffenburger, and Linda G. Griffith at the Biotechnology Process Engineering Center; Vicki Colvin and Kristen Kulinowski at the Center for Biological and Environmental Nanotechnology; Cyrus Shahabi, Farnoush Banaei-Kashani, Seon Kim, and Ugur Demiryurek of the Integrated Media Systems Center; Kyriacos A. Athanasiou, Joseph A. Kovach, David Balsley, Scott Keeney, Stanislao

Rizzo, Riccardo Santini, and Filippo Tenaglia; as well as many more ERC participants interviewed for our grant research whose names remain confidential. We also greatly appreciated comments and wisdom from Nish Acharya, Maura Arsiero, Gina A. Banks, Tom Byers, Michael C. Child, Arthur A. Ciocca, W. Dale Compton, Dean A. Cortopassi, Marc J. Epstein, Jerald Hage, Craig Hall, Benjamin F. Jones, David J. Kappos, David Karohl, Linda P. B. Katehi, Robert T. Keller, James Langer, Robert M. Nerem, Stephen G. Newberry, C. L. Max Nikias, Carl J. Schramm, Subra Suresh, Diether J. Recktenwald, and Matthew Wood.

We also wish to thank the outstanding publication team at Oxford University Press, who made the publication of the book a smooth and enjoyable process. Those individuals include Terry Vaughn, Scott Parris, Cathryn Vaulman, Melanie Mitzman, Balasubramanian Shanmugasundaram, and many others who worked behind the scenes to ensure a high-quality final product.

*Steven C. Currall* thanks Sara Jansen Perry, Emily M. Hunter, and Ed Frauenheim, who have been a dream come true as a research and writing team. I am deeply grateful for their insights, conscientiousness, and collaborative spirit. The idea for the grant for our research on ERCs came from Vicki Colvin. Subsequently, when I was on sabbatical as a visiting scholar at the University of Chicago's graduate school of business in 2003, I wrote the grant proposal and submitted it to Lynn Preston. The grant was refereed, and the award was made to me as the principal investigator with Toby E. Stuart, then a professor at the University of Chicago, also a member of the grant team and a deeply valued member of our group. I added Sara and Emily as researchers on the grant. I am grateful for support from the faculty and administrators at the University of Chicago, namely, Steve Kaplan, who was my faculty sponsor for the sabbatical; Ted Snyder, then the dean at the graduate school of business; and John Huizinga, then associate dean. As a sign of my gratitude to the NSF for supporting the research on which this book is based, I have elected to donate my royalty payments from the book to the NSF.

I also wish to thank a number of individuals who have been colleagues and supporters in my research and leadership of programs on innovation and entrepreneurship. Dan Watkins and Daryl Boudreaux were co-founders with me of the Rice Alliance for Technology and Entrepreneurship. Dan is a dear friend and has become the terrific venture capitalist that I knew he would. A special thank you to William and Stephanie Sick, who provided the endowment gift for the William and Stephanie Sick Professorship in Entrepreneurship in the Brown School of Engineering at Rice University, which I was honored to hold from 2001 to 2005. I could not have imagined a better partner than Brad Burke in growing the Rice Alliance. Jack M. Gill, the legendary forty-year investor in start-up companies and the human capital of young people, has been an invaluable colleague, mentor, friend, and advocate. The External Advisory Board of the Rice Alliance provided sage advice to me as founding director of the Rice Alliance. Members of the board were Robert Maxfield, Burton J. McMurtry, Bill Sick, Kenny Kurtzman, and Steve Lindsay. The Oversight Board of the Rice Alliance— C. Sidney Burrus, William H. Glick, Jordan Konisky, Kathleen S. Matthews, and the late Gilbert R. Whitaker—also provided wonderful support and guidance. The Alliance would not have been formed had it not been for the visionary support and initial funding of S. Malcolm Gillis, then president of Rice University. Eugene H. Levy, then provost at Rice, provided advice and financial support. David W. Leebron, current president of Rice, continued to provide a supportive environment for me. Dennis Murphree had the bright idea for our work together to launch what has become the Rice Business Plan Competition. Linda Werckle and Trish Leggett provided extraordinary support for the operations of the Alliance.

Neal Lane has been a sage advisor to me on an extraordinary number of topics, and I am immensely grateful for his friendship. I am inspired by James M. Tour, a genius scientist and dearest personal friend. Andrew R. Barron is a great colleague. The late Richard E. Smalley and Ken Kennedy were inspiring colleagues; their passing several years ago was a loss to the intellectual fabric of Rice. At University College London, Malcolm J. Grant, Bernard F. Buxton, and K. Michael Spyer could not have provided stronger support for my work to found the Department of Management Science and Innovation in the Faculty of Engineering Sciences and to found UCL Advances. Laura D. Tyson hired me at London Business School and provided unwavering advocacy of my work to strengthen entrepreneurship programs at the School.

Ralph J. Hexter, provost at the University of California, Davis (UC Davis), provided financial support for the writing of the book. I wish to thank my Organizational Behavior faculty colleagues at UC Davis for their useful suggestions during the early phase of the book-writing process: Beth Bechky, Nicole Woolsey Biggart, Gina Dokko, Kimberly D. Elsbach, Andrew B. Hargadon, Greta Hsu, and Donald A. Palmer. Also at UC Davis, Marianne Skoczek was superbly insightful and vigilant as a copy editor; Christina Lozano was our figure and table guru; Rodrigo Perez provided us with information technology tools to collaborate efficiently; and Tim Akin's marketing expertise is invaluable. My assistant, Nancy Enomoto, is a miracle worker and provides inexhaustible help to me every day. I appreciate the hard work of each of you during this process. Lastly, and most importantly, this book would not have been possible without the wisdom, support and patience of my dear wife, Cheyenne Currall.

*Ed Frauenheim* would like to thank his wife, Rowena, for her love, patience, and generous support during this project. You are my favorite innovation organizer. Thanks also to my son, Julius, and daughter, Skyla, for understanding all the time I had to spend "working." This is for you, Rowena, Julius, and Skyla. Thanks also to my colleagues at Human Capital Media, especially Rick Bell, for enabling me to devote time to finishing the book. A nod to my writing group for insights along the way. And lastly thanks to Steve, Emily, and Sara. Steve, thanks for the steady leadership and super project management. Sara, thanks for standing your ground even as you found common ground for the four of us. Emily, thanks for the "tough love" in the form of honest feedback and genuine enthusiasm. I'm proud to have been on the team.

*Sara Jansen Perry* would first like to thank my family, especially my supportive husband, Phillip, without whom I could not have devoted the time needed to this project. You are the ultimate collaborator in my life! I also thank my extraordinary coauthors, who made writing this book a fun and rewarding process. This book truly is "more than the sum of its parts" and a fine example of channeling management and social science curiosity to a place where it can have a broader impact. I'm honored to have been a part of it, I learned so much, and I treasure the unique connection I have with each of you. Lastly I would like to thank two important mentors in my professional career: Steve Currall and Alan Witt. I truly appreciate your investment in me.

*Emily Hunter* would like to extend gratitude to my coauthors. Steve provided vision and persistence; Ed lent his eloquence and quick wit; Sara kept us steady and lifted our spirits. Together we truly embodied the best of Boundary-Breaking Collaboration. And Sara, I am very blessed to have found such a true colleague and friend in you. I also thank Kendall Artz for his leadership and support, and Lisa Penney and Alan Witt for their guidance, mentoring, and friendship. Finally, I am eternally grateful to my husband and best friend, Louis, for everything.

# History and Impact of the Engineering Research Center Program

The ERC program got its start in 1985, during a time of deep anxiety about American economic competitiveness. Japanese car and electronic imports had raised concerns about US innovation and manufacturing capabilities. In addition, some US-based industry giants had commenced their retreat from extensive research and had, in some cases, shifted their focus to low costs as opposed to new features. The R&D gap discussed in chapter 2 opened and began to widen, exacerbating the competitiveness crisis.

At the same time, some US leaders in the sciences and engineering noticed a growing need to bridge research disciplines, improve the advancement of technology, and prepare engineering graduates better for industrial practice. In a 1983 report, the National Academy of Engineering—composed of academic and industry experts, including Academy President Robert White—called for greater interdisciplinary research.[1] They said government and industry should focus on cross-disciplinary activities in engineering as "major areas of concern."[2] They also cited faulty engineering education that failed to prepare students for practical careers. Among their concerns: inadequate hands-on experience that left undergraduates ill-prepared for jobs in industry or government.[3]

Against this backdrop, the National Science Foundation took action. It launched the Engineering Research Center program, defining it as a government-industry-university partnership aimed at strengthening the competitive position of US firms in world trade. The program had three primary goals: research, education, and partnerships with industry. With respect to research, the program from the outset recognized the importance of investigations that spanned traditional academic disciplines. It also was designed "to improve the education of engineers at all levels, and thereby increase the number of students who can contribute innovatively to US industry and its productivity."[4]

The initiative also aimed to close the gap between universities and industry. In a report about how to set up the ERC program, the National Academy of Engineering put this point in urgent terms. "[T]he relationships with industry must be real and must be perceived by both sides, the faculty and students of the Centers and the engineers and management of the participating companies, as mutually beneficial and as dealing with problems that are industrially important and intellectually demanding."[5]

The man who wrote those words had a good sense of the significance of these problems. He was W. Dale Compton, chairman of the panel created to give guidance on the ERCs and the then-vice president of research at Ford Motor Company. Compton and his peers could see the brewing troubles of declining corporate research. "There was the beginning of significant change in industrial research activities," Compton recalled in a recent interview. "They were becoming either extinct or they were changing from basic research to, essentially, development." Compton also knew they were up against an academic culture where scholars pursued projects largely on their own, without necessarily considering pressing problems facing industry. The program "required some philosophical change in both groups, both the basic researchers and the industry people who were involved."

In a number of ways, Compton was the perfect person to give the program its guiding principles. At Ford, his lab pioneered computer engine controls that boosted fuel efficiency. But he also had a background in academia. After earning a physics doctorate and working in a US Navy lab, Compton led the Coordinated Science Lab at the University of Illinois at Urbana-Champaign in the late 1960s. That experience not only grounded his perspective of academia's role in innovation but also made him a believer in interdisciplinary efforts. The lab marked an early example of bringing different kinds of researchers together, and doing so for real-world goals. Among the lab's achievements, for example, was the invention of air-based radar.

In his preface to the report advising NSF on how to structure the ERC program, Compton called for another feature that was in increasingly short supply in America: a long-term perspective. "Since this is a long-term program with results that will not be immediately demonstrable, all of the participants, including the government, must be patient and firm in maintaining funding for several years."[6] He and his peers had high hopes for the ERCs, stating, "If the Foundation embraces the concept with enthusiasm and supports it with zeal, the program could contribute well beyond expectations."[7]

ERCs IN PRACTICE

The NSF embraced the concept with some enthusiasm, investing roughly $1 billion in the ERC program over the past nearly thirty years. That is a drop in the federal budget bucket—Washington set aside nearly $7 billion for the National Science Foundation in 2011 alone. Still, some sixty centers had been funded as of 2012. In its operation, the ERC program has taken on the shape of the guidelines recommended by Compton's panel. For one thing, ERC funding for each center is large and lasts for an unusually long time. While the average length of NSF grants to individual researchers is 2.9 years, ERCs can receive money for up to ten years (originally for up to eleven).[8] And while the average amount of money given in NSF grants is less than $500,000, ERCs can expect to receive a total of $20 to $40 million. Center budgets can be supplemented by additional grants, fees, and donations from industry partners.

These industry partners are central to the operations of ERCs. Centers are expected to recruit a group of private sector companies that contribute funding and serve on an advisory board that helps determine research funding priorities. In a variety of other ways, ERCs work to include industry in their research and education efforts; this can take the form of frequent research update conference calls, intensive collaboration on research projects, and direct funding of particular experiments.

The program also created the *three-plane strategic planning framework,* a novel planning tool to ensure that ERCs envision technology systems that are high-risk, industrially important, and intellectually demanding. Under it, ERCs are expected to chart a course from the first plane of "fundamental knowledge" to a second plane of "enabling technologies" that allow the original insight to take practical form, and finally to a third plane of "engineered systems," which are effectively proofs-of-concept test beds or academic-scale prototypes.[9] The three-plane framework represents a holistic treatment of technology development. It calls for basic science and engineering research but puts those blue-sky efforts on a path to real-world products. Another way to describe it is a marriage of strategic planning and academic research. Center leaders are expected to assess the state of both the research and the commercial landscapes, and map out a set of experiments, refinements, and prototypes that are ready for the commercial realm, taken there by member firms or start-ups that champion them.

The three-plane framework is the brainchild of Lynn Preston, who has led the ERC program from its inception. Preston says the tool was a way to help organize academic researchers as they lead their centers. Especially when centers were not building a piece of hardware as their end-goal, many struggled with how to arrive at a technology system. The three-plane framework allowed researchers to see how to tie together basic research, the enabling technology pieces, and the systems-level result. "The thing that really works about it is it's so visual. . . . And it works across all sorts of technology fields," Preston says.

Preston developed the three-plane framework in the late 1990s, and it now guides ERC research programs. In particular, each ERC is expected to establish a number of research "thrusts" that can overlap but culminate in a number of "test beds" at the systems level where proofs-of-concept ideas are tested and prototypes are built. At the Center for Compact and Efficient Fluid Power at the University of Minnesota, for example, one of the thrusts is increasing the efficiency of fluid power systems—that is, machines that rely on liquid or gas pressure systems such as heavy construction equipment. Among the center's test beds is a high-efficiency excavator prototype, which relies on work accomplished in the efficiency thrust.

The focus on planning and delivery is enforced throughout the life of ERCs in a series of rigorous annual assessments by external review teams, led by NSF. Each year, ERCs must submit progress reports. What's more, in the third and sixth years, NSF review teams visit each center to assess achievements and evaluate updated research, test-bed plans, education, and industrial partnerships. ERCs are held to a high standard, and not all of them clear the bar. Nine centers have lost funding at some point for failing to fulfill program goals and expectations.

Preston supervises the centers with a kind of tough love. Some ERC directors and researchers see it as excessively tough at times, complaining that the program requires too much documentation. But the three-plane framework and the program overall generally receives praise from participants. Among the fans is Brad Bohlmann of the Center for Compact and Efficient Fluid Power. He says ERCs are a way to close the R&D gap in America. In fact, in Bohlmann's simple chart of that gap—discussed in chapter 2—he has a circle that intersects both the basic research of academia and product development of industry. He puts the letters "ERC" in that circle. Bohlmann says the chasm "needs to be filled by some methodology. The ERC program is one mechanism to achieve that goal, and it is effective."

## THE IMPACT OF ERCS

One of the most striking ways the ERC program has made a difference is through its emphasis on education. ERCs expose students more fully to the real-world practices of engineering. This happens in large part through frequent interaction with industry partners. The fluid power center, for example, has a webcast every other week in which graduate students from partner universities share their progress on different research projects. It is typical for industry partner officials to participate. The ERC Program's education emphasis has been on preparing graduates to come up to speed faster as they enter the industrial R&D workforce. It has also emphasized infusing engineering curricula with knowledge derived from each center's interdisciplinary projects. A 2006 NSF study found that 60 percent of the new courses introduced through ERCs had multidisciplinary content as well as a "systems" focus.[10] In 2008, the program began giving greater weight to creativity and innovation. Not only are students well-trained when they participate in an ERC, our research also found that students often acted as the glue connecting academics of different fields in ERCs. Students frequently carried out the experiments that bridged disciplines, forging links among themselves and among faculty members in various teams, disciplines, and even institutions.

What has been the impact of this ambitious educational strategy by ERCs? The result is a different kind of educational experience that produces a different kind of graduate. Studies repeatedly have found that students who were involved in ERCs emerge particularly well prepared for research and industry settings. A 2004 report from independent research firm SRI International found that nearly nine in ten company supervisors said former ERC students and graduates were better prepared to work in industry than equivalent hires without ERC experience. Nearly 75 percent of those supervisors said employees with ERC experience were better able to develop technology (see figure A.1).[11] Hiring students with ERC experience is one of the most prized benefits to companies working with the centers.[12]

Besides nurturing and encouraging a more engaged set of scientists, ERCs have produced a variety of other benefits for society. Companies, for example, profit in a range of ways from working with ERCs. A 1997 NSF report found that nearly a quarter of all firms reported having developed a new product or process as a result of their interaction with an ERC. A majority of the companies said ERC involvement had influenced their firm's research agenda. And, importantly, two-thirds reported that their firm's competitiveness had increased as a result of benefits received.[13]

A 2004 SRI International study found similar results. More than nine in ten ERC industry partners said obtaining access to new ideas and know-how was a significant benefit to them. And better than 70 percent said their involvement in the center boosted their competitiveness (see figure A.2).

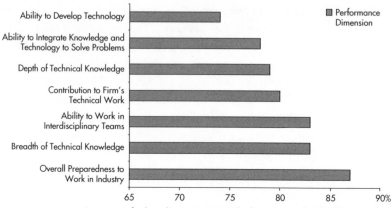

Percentage of industrial supervisors rating the former ERC students/graduates hired by their firms as "Better Than" or "Much Better Than" equivalent hires without ERC experience.

**Figure A.1: Performance of ERC Graduates with Non-ERC Hires: Comparisons by Member Firms**
Credit: ERC Program. Derived from SRI International, "Impact on Industry of Interaction with ERCs, Repeat Study," 2004.

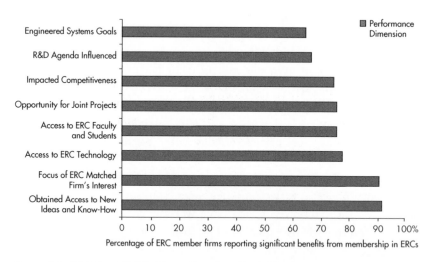

Percentage of ERC member firms reporting significant benefits from membership in ERCs

**Figure A.2: ERCs Provide Significant Benefit to Their Member Firms**
Credit: ERC Program. Derived from SRI International, "Impact on Industry of Interaction with ERCs, Repeat Study," 2004.

Overall, the return on investment to ERCs is striking. Although it is notoriously difficult to quantify the economic impact of research investments,[14] a 2010 NSF-commissioned study found that from 1985 through 2009, ERCs produced 1,701 invention disclosures, formal declarations of discoveries that often precede patents. In addition, ERCs had 624 patents awarded, granted 2,097 patent and software licenses, and spun off 142 firms with a cumulative total of 1,452 employees.[15]

The report, by Courtland Lewis of SciTech Communications, concluded that the ERC program had returned far more than the $1 billion invested in it. He emphasized "the total downstream market value of ERC innovations to the U.S. economy to date is well into the tens of billions of dollars, with some of the most promising technologies just now poised to begin rapid growth in the real-world market for technological goods and services."[16] These figures can't capture the centers' additional societal impacts, including improvements in human health, safety and security, environmental improvements, and quality of life.

Another recent assessment of ERCs' economic benefits by SRI International came to similar conclusions. In a close examination of five ERCs, the report discovered that one center in particular—the Center for Neuromorphic Systems Engineering (CNSE), based at Caltech—had a total quantifiable impact on the country of about $173 million. This benefit from CNSE, which focused on developing adaptive, sensing machines, represented a nearly sevenfold return on the federal government's investment of roughly $25 million.

Even so, SRI International researchers David Roessner, Lynne Manrique, and Jongwon Park warned that "focusing on narrowly conceived, quantifiable economic data alone should be avoided in these kinds of impact studies."[17] The authors found that another ERC, the Center for Power Electronics Systems (CPES) based at Virginia Tech, had quantifiable impacts of slightly more than $21 million on the US economy. But in the course of interviewing companies including Intel, General Electric, and International Rectifier, the authors concluded that the center had a much larger economic effect, one that could not be easily quantified. "Our interviews indicated that the actual impact of its central concept, modular integrated power systems for a variety of applications, almost certainly has amounted to multi-billion dollar benefits for the national economy."[18]

This study echoed the findings of other reports and experiences regarding the benefits students educated in ERCs provide upon graduation: "It is equally clear that CPES students have had very substantial economic impacts on the companies they work for, especially companies that have hired more than just a few of them. Those impacts, again according to our interviews, are attributable to the unique training they receive at CPES, notably involving systems thinking, multidisciplinary perspectives, and sensitivity to the industry context."[19]

Roessner, Manrique, and Park make another important observation: they note that ERCs often produce just a few "nuggets" in terms of discoveries, prototypes, and inventions that generate economic value. "Like a portfolio of venture investments, the proportion of ERC outputs that have realized significant, measurable economic impacts even after 10 years is quite small, perhaps two or three per center."[20]

The venture capital analogy is a fitting one. Few would doubt the value or wisdom of the US venture capital industry because it has a success rate of perhaps just 10 percent. That's because the return gained from the occasional hits can more than make up for the many failures—think of the stratospheric success of companies like Google, Facebook, and Twitter. ERCs ought to be viewed in the same way: each may not generate a huge number of commercial home runs, but they have consistently produced valuable breakthroughs.

To get another sense of the economic payoff of ERCs, consider the Microelectronics Packaging Research Center ERC based at the Georgia Institute of Technology. This ERC, which was funded from 1995 to 2006, focused on novel techniques for assembling electronics components. In particular, it pioneered *system-on-a-package* (SOP) technology to miniaturize electronic and bioelectronic systems for fields including the automotive, wireless, and military industries. The SOP concept involves a holistic approach to design and manufacturing of electronic systems, with integrated circuits, packages, system boards, and complete systems designed and developed for fabrication simultaneously. This contrasts with the prevailing manufacturing model, in which all the components were designed and built separately and then assembled together.

Motorola was one of this ERC's founding industrial partners and used parts of SOP technology in two models of its GSM/General Packet Radio Service quadband cellphones to realize about a 40 percent reduction in board area. The resulting module not only frees up space for new features but also serves as the base around which new mobile phones with different shapes and features—such as Bluetooth—can be rapidly designed. Motorola called its package a system-on-module (SOM), and had shipped tens of millions of SOM-based phones as of 2009.[21]

SRI International studied the overall return on investment of the Packaging Research Center to the Georgia economy in 2004. It found that the state of Georgia contributed $32.5 million to the center, while NSF put in another $32.7 million. The payoff for that investment totaled $351 million, including $192 million in direct benefits to the Georgia economy in the form of jobs, license fees, and consulting income, as well as $159 million in indirect ripple effects. Thus the ROI was more than $5 for every $1 spent, not including the economic benefit of several spinoff companies located outside Georgia or the ensuing value of the Motorola SOM-based phones.[22]

Another ERC that has had large financial impact is the Institute for Systems Research (ISR). This center, based at the University of Maryland at College Park, was funded from 1985 to 1994 and later extended through 1997. It conceived of satellite-based, two-way Internet connections to address the problem of large numbers of people worldwide who cannot access high-speed wired Internet connections. Working with Hughes Network Systems, ISR researchers developed hardware and software to "multicast" broadband data across satellites to homes and offices. The resulting HughesNet commercial offering generates about $1 billion annually to Hughes. The technology also has sparked a worldwide industry of other companies providing similar broadband services via satellite.

## EVOLVING FOR THE FUTURE

The ERC program has evolved over time. NSF officials heeded concerns that the initial centers tended not to tackle leading-edge topics because of the heavy emphasis on addressing industry's challenges. So the program created what were called Generation-2 and later Generation-3 centers designed to focus more attention on transformative research areas. In particular, NSF began making a distinction between "paradigmatic" and "pre-paradigmatic" centers. The former were focused on advancing the technology of an existing paradigm, or industry. The Center for Compact and Efficient Fluid Power at the University of Minnesota, which focuses on hydraulic and pneumatic technologies, is an example of a paradigmatic ERC. By contrast, pre-paradigmatic centers are intended to break ground in entirely new technology platforms and industries. The Biomimetic Microelectronic Systems ERC based at USC, which is working to establish the novel field of bioelectronics, represents this type of ERC.

Because of this shift over time, and because of a scarcity of grant monies overall, the ERC program has become one of the most sought-after research initiatives, says CBEN's Vicki Colvin. "They have become much, much more competitive and much, much more desirable. They're much, much more cutting-edge."

Preston also is convinced the program—and the three-plane framework in particular—have changed the mindset of American researchers.

"When I think about all the people who have wrapped their mind around that chart, I think we had a big intellectual impact in engineering, making people think more strategically, in a more integrative way."

## NOTES

1. National Academy of Engineering, *Strengthening Engineering*, 4.
2. Ibid., 5.
3. Ibid., 6.
4. National Academy of Engineering, *Guidelines for Engineering Research Centers*.
5. Ibid., vi.
6. Ibid., vii.
7. Ibid.
8. National Science Foundation, "NSF Funding Profile."
9. Engineering Research Centers, "Three-Plane Diagram."
10. Engineering Research Centers, "Summary of ERC Study Findings 2001–2008."
11. Ibid.
12. Parker, *Engineering Research Centers (ERC) Program*.
13. Ibid.
14. See Basken, "In Budget Battle."
15. Lewis, *Engineering Research Centers*.
16. Ibid.
17. Roessner, Manrique, and Park, "Economic Impact of Engineering Research Centers."
18. Ibid., 486.
19. Ibid.
20. Ibid., 481.
21. Engineering Research Centers, "Georgia Tech ERC."
22. Engineering Research Centers, "Summary of ERC Study Findings."

# APPENDIX B
# Research Methodology

## PURPOSE OF THE RESEARCH METHODOLOGY APPENDIX

We provide this technical appendix for the reader who is interested in how we came about developing the ideas in this book. To confirm that the material in this book is based on evidence rather than mere speculation, we wish to explain the nature of our research methods and the overarching research program. In the following sections we provide a summary of the methodological procedures we used to collect data and the sample of participants whose insights informed our conclusions.

## SUMMARY OF METHODOLOGICAL PROCEDURES

We used both quantitative and qualitative data collection methods to support this large-scale research program. The two methods were interwoven to maximize the knowledge yield of our research endeavor. Qualitative observation was used to understand the organizational context of ERCs and inductively articulate themes that describe the phenomena under study. Qualitative methods are particularly well suited for developing a grasp of organizational phenomena where a well-established body of research literature does not exist, as is the case with ERCs. Quantitative observation involves measuring the degree to which the phenomena under study actually exist and, subsequently, testing relationships among constructs.

Accordingly, we employed a two-phase design whereby we used qualitative methods (i.e., interviews, observations, and analysis of annual reports) to deepen our understanding of the organizational phenomenon under study and develop an accurate conceptualization of how ERCs are

**Table B.1.** TYPES OF DATA COLLECTED

| Type of Data | Level of Measurement | Level of Analysis | Use of Data |
|---|---|---|---|
| Interview | Individual | Individual | Context to generate hypotheses, survey, and explanation of findings |
| Survey | Individual | ERC and Individual | Individual perceptions, characteristics, and attitudes |
| Archival | ERC and Individual | ERC and Individual | Organizational outcomes and characteristics |

organized and how they operate. Then, during the quantitative phase, we used the information generated in the qualitative phase to develop and administer survey instruments. Also during the quantitative phase, we used objective information, gathered from archival data for five years prior and two years after the survey, to test our hypotheses. Thus, data were collected from three sources: interviews, surveys, and archival data. See table B.1 for a summary of the types of data collected, and the levels of measurement and analysis of each. By *levels of measurement,* we mean the level at which the data were collected. Individual-level measurement refers to data collected about individuals, which included archival, interview, and survey data collection. ERC-level measurement refers to ERC indices and ERC archival data from annual reports. *Levels of analysis* refers to the level at which the data was statistically analyzed. We analyzed data at the original level it was collected (i.e., both individual- and ERC-levels). We also aggregated all individual responses to ERC averages to analyze relationships of individual-level constructs with ERC-level outcomes.

## QUALITATIVE PHASE: INTERVIEW PARTICIPATION

In 2005 we visited eleven of the twenty-two operating National Science Foundation (NSF) Engineering Research Centers (ERCs) and conducted telephone interviews with at least one individual from each of the remaining eleven ERCs. See table B.2 for a full list of the twenty-two ERCs operating in 2005, all of which were included in our sample. ERCs were chosen for face-to-face visit based on their geographic location and willingness to host us for one to two days. In many cases, the director of the chosen ERCs

*Table B.2.* ERC TECHNOLOGY DESCRIPTIONS AND CATEGORIZATIONS

| ERC | Founding Year | Host University | Technology Area |
| --- | --- | --- | --- |
| ERC for Environmentally Benign Semiconductor Manufacturing | 1997 | University of Arizona | Manufacturing and processing |
| ERC for Extreme Ultraviolet Science and Technology | 2004 | Colorado State University | Microelectronic systems and information |
| Center for Neuromorphic Systems Engineering | 1995 | California Institute of Technology | Microelectronic systems and information |
| Mid-America Earthquake Center | 1998 | University of Illinois | Earthquake engineering |
| Center for Environmentally Beneficial Catalysis | 2004 | University of Kansas | Manufacturing and processing |
| ERC for Collaborative Adaptive Sensing of the Atmosphere | 2004 | University of Massachusetts | Manufacturing and processing |
| ERC for Biomimetic MicroElectronic Systems | 2004 | University of Southern California | Bioengineering |
| Particle Engineering Research Center | 1995 | University of Florida | Manufacturing and processing |
| Center for Low-Cost Electronic Packaging | 1995 | Georgia Institute of Technology | Manufacturing and processing |
| Biotechnology Process Engineering Center | 1995 | Massachusetts Institute of Technology | Bioengineering |
| ERC for Reconfigurable Manufacturing Systems | 1996 | University of Michigan | Manufacturing and processing |
| Integrated Media Systems Center | 1997 | University of Southern California | Microelectronic systems and information |
| Engineered Biomaterials ERC | 1997 | University of Washington | Bioengineering |
| Center for Advanced Engineering Fibers and Films | 1999 | Clemson University | Manufacturing and processing |
| ERC for Engineering of Living Tissues | 1999 | Georgia Tech | Bioengineering |
| Center for Computer-Integrated Surgical Systems and Technology | 1999 | Johns Hopkins University | Bioengineering |
| Center for Power Electronics Systems | 1999 | Virginia Tech | Microelectronic systems and information |
| Marine Bioproducts Engineering Center | 1998 | University of Hawaii | Bioengineering |

*continued*

**Table B.2.** (CONTINUED)

| ERC | Founding Year | Host University | Technology Area |
|---|---|---|---|
| VaNTH ERC for Bioengineering Education Technologies | 2000 | Vanderbilt University | Bioengineering |
| Center for Wireless Integrated MicroSystems | 2001 | University of Michigan | Microelectronic systems and information |
| Center for Subsurface Sensing and Imaging Systems | 2001 | Northeastern University | Microelectronic systems and information |
| Pacific Earthquake Engineering Research Center | 1998 | University of California, Berkeley | Earthquake engineering |
| Multidisciplinary Center for Earthquake Engineering Research | 1997 | University at Buffalo | Earthquake engineering |

had accepted an invitation to serve on a technical advisory board for this project. During each ERC interview visit, a wide variety of individuals were interviewed, including members of the leadership team, faculty, research thrust leaders, administrative staff, and graduate students. Interviews took place one-on-one or in groups, as appropriate. When the interviewee granted permission, we recorded interviews and referred to the tape recording to complete our notes for each interview. Additionally, in most cases, at least two researchers participated in every interview, with one research assistant attending every interview to maintain comparability across interviews. This procedure resulted in notes from the perspective of at least two researchers, in addition to the audiotapes. We ensured that our interpretations from each interview were accurate and consistent across interviewers.

Each interviewee was reminded that confidentiality would be maintained throughout the study. They were also informed that this research project was funded by a refereed grant, and was not contract research from NSF. This distinction allowed the research team more independence from NSF and ensured that the individual-level data collected will be kept confidential from NSF. Finally, interviewees were also reminded that only aggregated results would be shared with NSF, and no individuals would be identified. These three statements served to put the participants at ease and encourage them to respond candidly to the questions.

In addition to the interviews, members of the research team attended the annual conference for the ERC program in Washington, DC three years in a row (2004 to 2006). This conference provided ERC leaders the opportunity to share ideas, successes, and challenges. It also offered them developmental and informational seminars aimed at improving the management processes and innovation potential of all ERCs. As researchers, we attended a variety of sessions throughout the conferences and even participated in some sessions as presenters, which gave us better insight into the organizational context of ERCs. In total, considering the interviews and conferences, we devoted 135 person-hours to collecting qualitative data during the course of more than three years.

## QUANTITATIVE PHASE

### Survey Participation

The second phase of data collection consisted of administering an online survey in December 2005 to participants in all twenty-two ERCs. The survey was pilot tested in November 2005 to participants from another NSF-funded, university-based research center. After responses were received, a focus group was held to discuss reactions to the survey and its items. The survey was edited and finalized based on this feedback.

Then approximately 2,300 research faculty, center directors, industry partnering managers, administrative staff, graduate and undergraduate students, and postdoctoral researchers were invited to participate in an online survey (1,300 of these were nonstudents). In total, 839 people responded the survey (37 percent response rate). Among nonstudents, the response rate was also approximately 37 percent. After data cleaning, 380 respondents remained in the final sample. The demographics of the final sample are presented in table B.3.

The survey was comprised of approximately 120 questions. Whenever possible existing, prevalidated measures were included. To assess climate, we created items to fit our definitions of commercialization support and intra-organizational boundary-spanning climate based on our qualitative interviews (see table B.4). Confirmatory factor analysis results supported our hypothesized factor structure of these new scales, and climate was operationalized as an average of the nine items of each scale. (See Hunter, Perry, and Currall[1] for more information on measurement properties and aggregation).

**Table B.3.** DEMOGRAPHICS OF SURVEY RESPONDENTS

| Gender | Number | % of Total Respondents |
|---|---|---|
| Male | 285 | 75% |
| Female | 95 | 25% |

| Ethnicity | Number | % of Total Respondents |
|---|---|---|
| African American | 10 | 3% |
| Asian or Asian American | 65 | 17% |
| Hispanic | 23 | 6% |
| Native American | 1 | 0.3% |
| White/Caucasian | 267 | 70% |
| Other | 14 | 4% |

| Title at University | Number | % of Total Respondents |
|---|---|---|
| Professor/lecturer | 225 | 59% |
| Department chair or dean | 12 | 3% |
| Administrative staff | 40 | 11% |
| Research scientist/support personnel | 35 | 9% |
| Postdoctoral researcher | 10 | 3% |
| Student | 90 | 24% |
| Other | 30 | 8% |

| Role at ERC | Number | % of Total Respondents |
|---|---|---|
| Director (faculty) | 18 | 5% |
| Assistant director | 27 | 7% |
| Administrative director | 18 | 5% |
| Industrial liaison officer | 15 | 4% |
| Educational/outreach director | 20 | 5% |
| Testbed leader (faculty) | 14 | 4% |
| Thrust leader (faculty) | 45 | 12% |
| Project leader (faculty) | 68 | 18% |
| Other leadership role | 28 | 7% |
| General faculty member (no leadership role) | 81 | 21% |
| Support staff | 14 | 4% |
| Postdoctoral researcher | 10 | 3% |
| Graduate student | 85 | 22% |
| Undergraduate student | 5 | 1% |
| Other | 51 | 13% |

*Note*: Survey respondents were allowed to select more than one category when describing their position and role within their ERC

**Table B.4.** CLIMATE SURVEY ITEMS

| Construct | Scales[a] | Items |
|---|---|---|
| Commercialization-Support Climate | Perceptions of commercialization-support from ERC | Commercialization of ERC research is encouraged . . ,<br>1. . . . in my ERC.<br>2. . . . at my university (i.e., where I hold my main employment).<br>3. . . . in my home academic department. |
| | Perceptions of commercialization-support from ILO | The industrial liaison officer (ILO) in my ERC . . .<br>1. . . . assists faculty with commercialization processes.<br>2. . . . successfully encourages faculty members to become involved in the process of commercialization. |
| | Perceptions of commercialization-support from TTO | The Office of Technology Transfer (or Licensing) at my university is . . .<br>1. . . . easy to work with in the process of commercialization.<br>2. . . . effective in carrying out its responsibilities in the process of commercialization. |
| | Perceptions of commercialization-support from university community | In launching start-up companies, . . .<br>1. . . . management talent is available to assist researchers in my ERC.<br>2. . . . incubator services are available to assist researchers in my ERC. |

*continued*

*Table B.4.* (CONTINUED)

| Construct | Scales[a] | Items |
|---|---|---|
| Intra-Organizational Boundary-Spanning Climate | Perceptions of degree of collaboration (e.g., among thrusts) | 1. Collaboration (e.g., research, publications) occurs among the projects within each thrust[b] |
| | | 2. Collaboration (e.g., research, publications) occurs among thrusts. |
| | | 3. My involvement with students and/or postdocs increases my collaboration (e.g., research, publications) with people in other thrusts. |
| | Perceptions of organizational structures promoting collaboration | 1. Collaboration (e.g., research, publications) occurs among project teams that operate on different levels of the three-plane framework. |
| | | 2. My ERC has a formal committee or team devoted to promoting collaboration across the thrusts. |
| | | 3. The thrusts are structured in such a way that requires collaboration across levels of the three-plane framework. |
| | | 4. The project teams are structured in such a way that requires collaboration across levels of the three-plane framework. |
| | Perceptions of multi-disciplinary research | 1. Within the thrusts in my ERC, multidisciplinary research is carried out. |
| | | 2. The structure of thrusts has evolved over time in order to remain focused on multidisciplinary research. |

[a] All scales used 7-point response scale, anchored from "Strongly Disagree" to "Strongly Agree."
[b] A thrust is a research team with a shared broad research objective, within which there are numerous specific project groups.
Reproduced with permission: Emily M. Hunter, Sara Jansen Perry, and Steven C. Currall, "Inside Multi-Disciplinary Science and Engineering Research Centers: The Impact of Organizational Climate on Invention Disclosures and Patents," *Research Policy* 40, no. 9 (November 2011): 1226–39.

## ARCHIVAL REPORTS

Each year, all ERCs must report their financial and performance data to a third party company with whom NSF contracts to collect, organize, and analyze ERC data. For our study, we collected archival data from this third party company for all twenty-two active ERCs. We also received paper or electronic copies of the full annual narrative reports submitted to NSF by all ERCs. Together, these data provided many organizational outcome indicators (e.g., patents, publications, and new courses created) and they also added to our contextual knowledge regarding the activities, resources, personnel, and performance of each ERC (e.g., funding, industry partners, budgets). See Perry, Currall, and Stuart[2] for a full listing of ERC funding sources and technology/knowledge transfer outputs, as well as other information about the ERCs participating in this research.

In summary, the research program that spurred this book is an ongoing, large-scale, multi-method effort. The researchers were careful to employ robust, reliable, and valid research methods. The results of these efforts provide important insight into the themes discussed in this book.

## NOTES

1. Hunter, Perry, and Currall, "Inside Multi-Disciplinary Science and Engineering Research Centers."
2. Perry, Currall, and Stuart, "Pipeline from University Laboratory."

APPENDIX C

# Research Questions for Future Scholarly Examinations of Organized Innovation

The following are examples of research questions derived from the Organized Innovation framework that future scholars may wish to test empirically:

1. What are the requisite skills that leaders of multidisciplinary research centers must demonstrate to foster Channeled Curiosity, Boundary-Breaking Collaboration, and Orchestrated Commercialization?
2. Can such leadership skills be embodied in a single leader? Channeled Curiosity emphasizes orienting, Boundary-Breaking Collaboration emphasizes facilitating, and Orchestrated Commercialization emphasizes coordinating. Can all those activities be fulfilled by one person or is a team of leaders with different skills required?
3. What leadership experience and/or mentorship programs should university leaders put in place to develop a pool of faculty members and other leaders who are able to apply the principles of Organized Innovation?
4. What policies and procedures are necessary to create an organizational climate at multidisciplinary research centers that serves as the foundation for Organized Innovation? What obstacles do centers face if the current climate needs to be altered? What organizational support structures or processes can help leaders overcome those obstacles?
5. What are the optimal incentive schemes to foster application of Organized Innovation principles? Is it possible to use financial incentives to encourage Channeled Curiosity and Boundary-Breaking Collaboration, or must financial incentives be reserved solely for Orchestrated

Commercialization? Are nonfinancial incentives more appropriate for Channeled Curiosity and Boundary-Breaking Collaboration, such as prizes or citations for university faculty who demonstrate those actions?

6. Are role models more powerful than formal incentives of any type in compelling behaviors that are consistent with the Organized Innovation framework?

7. What training is required to equip researchers with the skills necessary to advance the Organized Innovation framework? For example, how should universities ensure that researchers and/or center leaders have the basic skills of communication and conflict resolution that are required of, for example, Boundary-Breaking Collaboration?

8. What entrepreneurial behaviors do researchers need to fully display to create an organization embodying the Organized Innovation framework?

9. What are the appropriate economic measures of success of any Organized Innovation initiative (e.g., companies formed, jobs created, new products introduced to the marketplace)? What are the quantitative and qualitative measures that can be used to assess return on investment of the Organized Innovation framework?

10. What indicators of societal impact (e.g., non-economic) should be used to further measure return on investment in Organized Innovation-based initiatives?

11. What metrics or measures are appropriate to assess organizational levels of Channeled Curiosity, Boundary-Breaking Collaboration, and Orchestrated Commercialization?

# BIBLIOGRAPHY

Adams, J. S. "The Structure and Dynamics of Behavior in Organizational Boundary Roles." In *Handbook of Industrial and Organizational Psychology*, edited by M. D. Dunnette and L. M. Hough, 1175–99. Palo Alto, CA: Consulting Psychologists Press, 1976.

American Chemical Society. "Discovery and Development of Penicillin, 1928–1945," accessed April 19, 2013. http://portal.acs.org/portal/acs/corg/content?_nfpb=true&_pageLabel=PP_SUPERARTICLE&node_id=520&use_sec=false&sec_url_var=region1&__uuid=5cee831f-65ae-426f-9b49-4edc2515bdef.

Anthony, Scott D. "The New Corporate Garage." *Harvard Business Review*, September 2012.

Apple. "Jobs at Apple: Process Engineer-Camera," accessed September 5, 2012. http://jobs.apple.com/index.ajs?BID=1&method=mExternal.showJob&RID=88533&CurrentPage=1.

Association of University Technology Managers. *AUTM Transaction Survey FY2009*. Deerfield, IL: Association of University Technology Managers, 2011.

Augustine, Norman R. "America's Competitiveness." Testimony before the Democratic Steering and Policy Committee, US House of Representatives, January 7, 2009. http://www.aau.edu/WorkArea/showcontent.aspx?id=8154.

Baker, Stephen. "Putting a Price on Social Connections." *Bloomberg Businessweek*, April 8, 2009. http://www.businessweek.com/stories/2009-04-08/putting-a-price-on-social-connectionsbusinessweek-business-news-stock-market-and-financial-advice.

Basken, Paul. "In Budget Battle, Science Faces New Pressures to Show It Delivers." *Chronicle of Higher Education*, November 23, 2012.

Bauerlein, Mark, Mohamed Gad-el-Hak, Wayne Grody, Bill McKelvey, and Stanley W. Trimble. "We Must Stop the Avalanche of Low-Quality Research." *Chronicle of Higher Education*, June 13, 2010. http://chronicle.com/article/We-Must-Stop-the-Avalanche-of/65890.

Bercovitz, Janet, and Maryann Feldman. "Academic Entrepreneurs: Organizational Change at the Individual Level." *Organization Science* 19, no. 1 (January/February 2008): 69–89.

Boardman, Craig, and Denis Gray. "The New Science and Engineering Management: Cooperative Research Centers as Government Policies, Industry Strategies and Organizations." *Journal of Technology Transfer* 35, no. 5 (2010): 445–59.

Bowen, H. Kent, Alex Kazaks, Ayr Muir-Harmony, and Bryce LaPierre. *The Langer Lab: Commercializing Science,* Case 605–017. Boston: Harvard Business School, 2004, rev. 2005.

Bown, Stephen R. *A Most Damnable Invention: Dynamite, Nitrates, and the Making of the Modern World.* New York: Thomas Dunne Books, 2005.

Breakthrough Institute. "Interview with Dan Steward, Former Mitchell Energy Vice President," December 20, 2011. http://thebreakthrough.org/blog/2011/12/interview_with_dan_steward_for.shtml.

Brooks, David. "Where Are the Jobs?" *New York Times,* October 6, 2011. http://www.nytimes.com/2011/10/07/opinion/brooks-where-are-the-jobs.html.

Carswell, Lindsay. "Build a Liver." ScienceCentral, accessed February 25, 2013. http://www.sciencentral.com/articles/view.php3?article_id=218392284.

Casey, Joseph, and Katherine Koleski. *Backgrounder: China's 12th Five-Year Plan.* Washington, DC: U.S.-China Economic and Security Review Commission, 2011. http://origin.www.uscc.gov/sites/default/files/Research/12th-FiveYear-Plan_062811.pdf.

Cassidy, John. "Enter the Dragon." *New Yorker,* December 13, 2010.

Cassidy, John. *How Markets Fail: The Logic of Economic Calamities.* New York: Farrar, Straus and Giroux, 2010.

Center for Compact and Efficient Fluid Power "About Us," accessed April 19, 2013. http://www.ccefp.org/about-us.

Chesbrough, Henry. *Open Business Models: How to Thrive in the New Innovation Landscape.* Boston: Harvard Business Review Press, 2006.

Chronicle of Higher Education, *Almanac, 2013–2014,* Special issue, 59, no. 46 (2013): 57.

Clegg, Chris, Kerrie Unsworth, Olga Epitropaki, and Giselle Parker. "Implicating Trust in the Innovation Process." *Journal of Occupational and Organizational Psychology* 75 (2002): 409–22.

Cohen, I. Bernard, and George E. Smith. Introduction to *The Cambridge Companion to Newton.* Cambridge: Cambridge University Press, 2002.

Collins, Jim, and Morten T. Hansen. *Great by Choice: Uncertainty, Chaos, and Luck—Why Some Thrive Despite Them All.* New York: HarperBusiness, 2011.

Colvin, Geoff. *Talent Is Overrated: What Really Separates World-Class Performers from Everybody Else.* New York: Portfolio, 2008.

Committee on a New Biology for the 21st Century. *A New Biology for the 21st Century.* Washington, DC: National Academies Press, 2009. http://www.nap.edu/openbook.php?record_id=12764&page=1.

Committee on Research Universities, Board on Higher Education and Workforce, Policy and Global Affairs, and National Research Council. *Research Universities and the Future of America: Ten Breakthrough Actions Vital to our Nation's Prosperity and Security.* Washington, DC: National Academies Press, 2012.

Cone, Judith. *Progress Report Year Two of Five-Year Plan: Strategic Roadmap to Accelerate Innovation at the University of North Carolina at Chapel Hill.* Chapel Hill: University of North Carolina, Chapel Hill, Chancellor's Office, 2012. http://innovate.unc.edu/site/wp-content/uploads/2012/10/FINAL-report-PDF.pdf.

Currall, Steven C. "Stewarding the University of California Dream." Huffington Post, accessed June 29, 2013. http://www.huffingtonpost.com/steve-currall/university-of-california-_b_2224257.html.

Currall, Steven C., and Marc J. Epstein. "The Fragility of Organizational Trust: Lessons from the Rise and Fall of Enron." *Organizational Dynamics* 32 (2003): 193–206.

Currall, Steven C., and Andrew C. Inkpen. "On the Complexity of Organizational Trust: A Multi-level Co-Evolutionary Perspective and Guidelines for Future Research." In *The Handbook of Trust Research*, edited by Reinhard Bachmann and Akbar Zaheer, 235–46. Cheltenham, UK: Edward Elgar, 2006.

Currall, Steven C., and Timothy A. Judge. "Measuring Trust between Organizational Boundary Role Persons." *Organizational Behavior and Human Decision Processes* 64 (1995): 151–70.

Currall, Steven C., Eden B. King, Neal Lane, Juan Madera, and Stacey Turner. "What Drives Public Acceptance of Nanotechnology?" *Nature Nanotechnology* 1 (2006): 153–55.

Cuttino, Phyllis. "America Needs Clean Energy Support." Pew Charitable Trusts, December 7, 2011. http://www.pewenvironment.org/news-room/opinions/america-needs-clean-energy-support-85899367143.

Cyranoski, David, Natasha Gilbert, Heidi Ledford, Anjali Nayar, and Mohammed Yahia. "Education: The PhD Factory." *Nature*, April 20, 2011. http://www.nature.com/news/2011/110420/full/472276a.html.

Dooley, J. J. *U.S. Federal Investments in Energy R&D: 1961–2008*, PNNL 17952. Richland, WA: Pacific Northwest National Laboratory, 2008. http://www.pnl.gov/main/publications/external/technical_reports/PNNL-17952.pdf.

Duhigg, Charles, and Keith Bradsher. "How the U.S. Lost Out on iPhone Work." *New York Times,* January 21, 2012. http://www.nytimes.com/2012/01/22/business/apple-america-and-a-squeezed-middle-class.html?pagewanted=all.

Dyer, Jeffrey H., and Chu Wujin. "The Role of Trustworthiness in Reducing Transaction Costs and Improving Performance: Empirical Evidence from the United States, Japan, and Korea." *Organization Science* 14 (2003): 57–68.

Dyer, Jeffrey, Hal Gregersen, and Clayton Christensen. *The Innovator's DNA: Mastering the Five Skills of Disruptive Innovators*. Boston: Harvard Business Review Press, 2011.

*Economist.* "Gas Works," July 14, 2012. http://www.economist.com/node/21558459.

*Economist.* "A New Idolatry: Shareholders v. Stakeholders," April 24, 2010.

*Economist.* "Special Report: America's Competitiveness," March 16, 2013.

Einhorn, Bruce, and Michael Arndt. "The 25 Most Innovative Companies 2010." *Bloomberg Businessweek,* April 15, 2010. http://images.businessweek.com/ss/10/04/0415_most_innovative_companies/index.htm?chan=magazine+channel_special+report.

Einhorn, Bruce, and Michael Arndt. "The 50 Most Innovative Companies." *Bloomberg Businessweek,* April 15, 2010. http://www.businessweek.com/magazine/content/10_17/b4175034779697.htm.

Engineering Research Centers. "Georgia Tech ERC Pioneered System-on-a-Package Concept," accessed October 26, 2012. http://www.erc-assoc.org/docs/graduated_centers/GaTech%20PRC-Retrospect-SOP_CL-LPedit.pdf.

Engineering Research Centers. "Summary of ERC Study Findings 2001–2008," accessed April 24, 2013. http://www.erc-assoc.org/studies_and_reports.

Engineering Research Centers. "Three-Plane Diagram," accessed October 26, 2012. http://www.erc-assoc.org/content/three-plane-diagram.

European Commission. "R & D Expenditure," accessed September 5, 2012. http://epp.eurostat.ec.europa.eu/statistics_explained/index.php/R_%26_D_expenditure.

Eurostat. "Gross Domestic Expenditure on R&D (GERD)," accessed September 5, 2012. http://epp.eurostat.ec.europa.eu/tgm/table.do?tab=table&init=1&plugin=1&language=en&pcode=t2020_20.

Ewing Marion Kauffman Foundation. "Proof of Concept Centers," accessed April 15, 2013. http://www.kauffman.org/advancing-innovation/proof-of-concept-centers.aspx.

Fauber, John. "Drug Research Routinely Suppressed, Study Authors Find." *Milwaukee Journal Sentinel*, January 3, 2012. http://www.jsonline.com/features/health/drug-research-routinely-suppressed-study-authors-find-qd3kfnn-136625848.html.

Feller, Irwin, Catherine P. Ailes, and J. David Roessner. "Impacts of Research Universities on Technological Innovation in Industry: Evidence from Engineering Research Centers." *Research Policy* 31, no. 2 (March 2002): 457–74.

Fogel, Daniel Mark, and Elizabeth Malson-Huddle. *Precipice or Crossroads? Where America's Great Universities Stand and Where They Are Going Midway through Their Second Century.* Albany: State University of New York Press, 2012.

Frauenheim, Ed. "Bringing the Jobs Back Home: How 'Re-shoring' Is Coming to America." Workforce.com, February 7, 2013. http://www.workforce.com/article/20130207/NEWS02/130209984/bringing-the-jobs-back-home-how-re-shoring-is-coming-to-america#.

Frauenheim, Ed. "Delayed Innovation Gratification." Work in Progress (blog), WorkForce.com, November 29, 2012. http://www.workforce.com/article/20121129/BLOGS05/121129968/delayed-innovation-gratification.

Frauenheim, Ed. "When 'Agility' Adopts the Symptoms of A.D.D." Work in Progress (blog), WorkForce.com, January 13, 2013. http://www.workforce.com/article/20120113/BLOGS05/120119976/when-agility-adopts-the-symptoms-of-a-d-d#.

Fraunhofer-Gesellschaft. "Tailor-Made Light," accessed September 5, 2012. http://www.fraunhofer.de/en/research-topics/production-and-environment/special-theme/laser-technology.html.

Friedman, Thomas L. "Need a Job? Invent It," *New York Times,* accessed July 19, 2013, http://www.nytimes.com/2013/03/31/opinion/sunday/friedman-need-a-job-invent-it.html.

Friedman, Thomas L. "The Amazing Energy Race," *New York Times*, accessed July 19, 2013, http://www.nytimes.com/2013/07/03/opinion/friedman-the-amazing-energy-race.html.

Friedman, Thomas L., and Michael Mandelbaum. *That Used to Be Us: How America Fell Behind in the World It Invented and How We Can Come Back.* New York: Farrar, Straus and Giroux, 2011.

Gap International. "Competition or Collaboration? Building Interdependence to Increase Sales Effectiveness," webinar, July 20, 2010. http://www.slideshare.net/GapInternational/gap-international-interdependence-a.

General Electric. *GE Global Innovation Barometer 2011: An Overview on Messaging, Data and Amplification.* Accessed September 5, 2012. http://files.gereports.com/wp-content/uploads/2011/01/GIB-results.pdf.

Gertner, Jon. *The Idea Factory: Bell Labs and the Great Age of American Innovation.* New York: Penguin, 2012.

Gertner, Jon "True Innovation." *New York Times,* February 25, 2012. http://www.nytimes.com/2012/02/26/opinion/sunday/innovation-and-the-bell-labs-miracle.html?_r=1&ref=opinion&pagewanted=all.

Gladwell, Malcolm. *Outliers: The Story of Success.* New York: Little, Brown, 2008.

Golde, Chris M., and Hanna Alix Gallagher. "The Challenges of Conducting Interdisciplinary Research in Traditional Doctoral Programs." *Ecosystems* (July 1999): 281. http://chris.golde.org/filecabinet/ecosystem.pdf.

Goode, Erica. "How Culture Molds Habits of Thought." *New York Times,* August 8, 2000. http://www.nytimes.com/2000/08/08/science/how-culture-molds-habits-of-thought.html?pagewanted=all&src=pm.

Grove, Andy. "How America Can Create Jobs." *Bloomberg Businessweek*, July 1, 2010. http://www.businessweek.com/magazine/content/10_28/b4186048358596.htm.

Hage, Jerald. *Restoring the Innovative Edge: Driving the Evolution of Science and Technology.* Palo Alto, CA: Stanford University Press, 2011.

Hale, Katherine. "Collaboration in Academic R&D: A Decade of Growth in Pass-Through Funding." *InfoBrief* (National Center for Science Engineering Statistics/National Science Foundation), August 2012. http://www.nsf.gov/statistics/infbrief/nsf12325/#note2.

Hamel, Gary. *What Matters Now.* San Francisco: Jossey-Bass, 2012.

Hamilton, David P. "Publishing by—and for?—the Numbers." *Science* 250 (December 7, 1990): 1331–32.

Hargadon, Andrew. *How Breakthroughs Happen: The Surprising Truth about How Companies Innovate.* Boston: Harvard Business School Press, 2003.

Hargadon, Andrew. "Sustaining Innovation." Unpublished manuscript, 2012.

Henneman, Todd. "Not Your Grandfather's Industrial Lab." Workforce.com, January 17, 2013. http://www.workforce.com/article/20130117/NEWS02/130119953/not-your-grandfathers-industrial-lab#.

Hourihan, Matt. "Historical Trends in Federal R&D." Chap. 2 in *AAAS Report XXXVII Research and Development FY 2013.* Washington, DC: American Association for the Advancement of Science, 2012. http://www.aaas.org/spp/rd/rdreport2013/13pch02.pdf.

http://www.claytonchristensen.com/key-concepts/

Hunter, Emily M., Sara Jansen Perry, and Steven C. Currall. "Inside Multi-Disciplinary Science and Engineering Research Centers: The Impact of Organizational Climate on Invention Disclosures and Patents." *Research Policy* 40, no. 9 (November 2011): 1226–39.

Imperial Innovations. "About Imperial Innovations," accessed April 22, 2013. http://www.imperialinnovations.co.uk/about.

Intersociety Working Group. *AAAS Report XXXVII: Research and Development FY 2013.* Washington, DC: American Association for the Advancement of Science, 2013. http://www.aaas.org/spp/rd/rdreport2013.

Isaacson, Walter. *Steve Jobs.* New York: Simon & Schuster, 2011.

Jaruzelski, Barry, Matthew Le Merle, and Sean Randolph. *The Culture of Innovation: What Makes San Francisco Bay Area Companies Different?* San Francisco: Bay Area Council Economic Institute and Booz and Co., 2012.

Jensen, Richard, and Marie Thursby. "Proofs and Prototypes for Sale: The Licensing of University Inventions." *American Economic Review* 91, no. 1 (March 2001): 240–59.

Kammenm, Daniel M., and Gregory F. Nemet. "Reversing the Incredible Shrinking Energy R&D Budget." *Issues in Science and Technology* (Fall 2005). http://www.issues.org/22.1/realnumbers.html.

Karlberg, Johan P. E. "Biomedical Publication Trends by Geographic Area." *Clinical Trial Magnifier* 2, no. 12 (December 2009): 682–701.

Langer, James S. "Enabling Scientific Innovation." *Science* 338, no. 6104 (October 12, 2012): 171.

Lewis, Courtland S. *Engineering Research Centers: Innovations—ERC-Generated Commercialized Products, Processes, and Startups.* Arlington, VA: National Science Foundation, 2010. http://www.erc-assoc.org/topics/policies_studies/ ERC%20Innovations%202010-final.pdf.

Lowrey, Annie "High-Tech Factories Built to Be Engines of Innovation." *New York Times,* December 13, 2012. http://www.nytimes.com/2012/12/14/business/ companies-see-high-tech-factories-as-fonts-of-ideas.html?_r=0.

Malakoff, David. "The Many Ways of Making Academic Research Pay Off." *Science* 339 no. 6121 (February 15, 2013): 750–53.

Maseeh Entrepreneurship Prize Competition. "About the Prize," accessed April 22, 2013. http://maseeh.usc.edu/theprize.php.

Mervis, Jeffrey. "Suresh Leaves His Mark on NSF as He Heads to Carnegie Mellon." *Science,* 339, no. 6126 (March 22, 2013): 1380–81.

Mowery, David C., Richard R. Nelson, Bhaven N. Sampat, and Arvids A. Ziedonis. "The Growth of Patenting and Licensing by U.S. Universities: An Assessment of the Effects of the Bayh—Dole Act of 1980." *Research Policy* 30 (2001): 99–119.

Myers, David R., Carol W. Sumpter, Steven T. Walsh, and Bruce A. Kirchhoff. "A Practitioner's View: Evolutionary Stages of Disruptive Technologies." *IEEE Transactions on Engineering Management* 49, no. 4 (2002): 322–29.

National Academies. "In National Academy of Sciences Speech, President Obama Announces Major Investments in Research and Education, Encourages NAS Members to Think about New Ways to Engage Young People in Science," news release, April 27, 2009. http://www8.nationalacademies.org/onpinews/ newsitem.aspx?RecordID=20090427.

National Academies. *Rising above the Gathering Storm: Energizing and Employing America for a Brighter Economic Future.* Washington, DC: National Academies Press, 2007.

National Academies. *Rising above the Gathering Storm, Revisited: Rapidly Approaching Category 5.* Washington, DC: National Academies Press, 2010.

National Academy of Engineering. *Guidelines for Engineering Research Centers.* Washington, DC: National Academy of Engineering, 1983.

National Academy of Engineering. *Strengthening Engineering in the National Science Foundation.* Washington, DC: National Academy of Engineering, 1983.

National Aeronautics and Space Administration. "Reliving the Wright Way," accessed April 18, 2013. http://wright.nasa.gov/index.htm.

National Science Board. "National Science Board Releases Science and Engineering Indicators 2010," news release, January 15, 2010. http://www.nsf.gov/news/ news_summ.jsp?cntn_id=116238.

National Science Board. *Science and Engineering Indicators 2012.* Arlington, VA: National Science Foundation, 2012. http://www.nsf.gov/statistics/seind12.

National Science Foundation. *National Patterns of R&D Resources: 2008 Data Update,* NSF 10–314. Arlington, VA: National Science Foundation, 2010. http://www. nsf.gov/statistics/nsf10314/.

National Science Foundation. "NSF Funding Profile," accessed October 26, 2012. http://www.nsf.gov/about/budget/fy2013/pdf/04_fy2013.pdf.

O'Shea, R. P., H. Chugh, and T. J. Allen. "Determinants and Consequences of University Spinoff Activity: A Conceptual Framework." *Journal of Technology Transfer* 33, no. 6 (2008): 653–66.

Our Documents. "Transcript of Morrill Act (1862)," accessed April 19, 2013. http://www.ourdocuments.gov/doc.php?flash=true&doc=33&page=transcript.

Owen-Smith, Jason, and Walter W. Powell. "The Expanding Role of University Patenting in the Life Sciences: Assessing the Importance of Experience and Connectivity." *Research Policy* 32 (2003): 1695–11.

Parker, Linda. *The Engineering Research Centers (ERC) Program: An Assessment of Benefits and Outcomes.* Arlington, VA: National Science Foundation, 1997. http://www.nsf.gov/pubs/1998/nsf9840/nsf9840.htm.

Nurse, Paul, Richard Treisman, and Jim Smith. "Building Better Institutions." *Science* 341 (2013): 10.

Pentland, William. "The Top Cleantech Countries." Forbes.com, December 6, 2010. http://www.forbes.com/2010/12/02/china-germany-japan-america-business-energy-ecotech-clean-tech-patents.html.

Perry, Sara Jansen, Steven C. Currall, and Toby E. Stuart. "The Pipeline from University Laboratory to New Commercial Product: An Organizational Framework Regarding Technology Commercialization in Multidisciplinary Research Centers." In *The Creative Enterprise*, edited by Tony Davila, Marc J. Epstein, and Robert D. Shelton, 85–105. Westport, CT: Praeger, 2007.

Pew Charitable Trusts. *Who's Winning the Clean Energy Race? 2010 Edition.* Philadelphia and Washington, DC: Pew Charitable Trusts, 2011. http://www.pewenvironment.org/uploadedFiles/PEG/Publications/Report/G-20Report-LOWRes-FINAL.pdf.

Pomfret, John. "China Pushing the Envelope on Science, and Sometimes Ethics." *Washington Post*, June 28, 2010. http://www.washingtonpost.com/wp-dyn/content/article/2010/06/27/AR2010062703639_pf.html.

President's Council of Advisors on Science and Technology (PCAST). *Transformation and Opportunity: The Future of the U.S. Research Enterprise.* Washington, DC: President's Council of Advisors on Science and Technology, 2012. http://www.whitehouse.gov/sites/default/files/microsites/ostp/pcast_future_research_enterprise_20121130.pdf.

Ramanujam, Vasudevan, N. Venkatraman, and John C. Camillus. "Multi-Objective Assessment of Effectiveness of Strategic Planning: A Discriminant Analysis Approach." *Academy of Management Journal* 29, no. 2 (1986): 347–72.

Ramirez, Jessica. "Lucky Discoveries." *Newsweek*, August 31, 2010. http://www.thedailybeast.com/newsweek/galleries/2010/08/31/famous-accidental-discoveries.html.

Rice University Business Plan Competition. "2012 Rice Business Plan Competition Awards $1.55 Million in Prizes—Richest Ever," accessed April 22, 2013. http://alliance.rice.edu/2012_Participant_Winners.

Roberts, Edward B. *Entrepreneurs in High Technology: Lessons from MIT and Beyond.* New York: Oxford University Press, 1991.

Roessner, David, Lynne Manrique, and Jongwon Park. "The Economic Impact of Engineering Research Centers: Preliminary Results of a Pilot Study." *Journal of Technology Transfer* 35, no. 5 (October 2010): 475–93.

Schacht, Wendy H. *Industrial Competitiveness and Technological Advancement: Debate Over Government Policy.* Washington, DC: Congressional Research Service, 2009. http://fpc.state.gov/documents/organization/133893.pdf.

Schneider, B., S. S. White, and M. C. Paul. "Linking Service Climate and Customer Perceptions of Service Quality: Test of a Causal Model." *Journal of Applied Psychology* 83 (1998): 150–64.

Shane, Scott, and Toby E. Stuart. "Organizational Endowments and the Performance of University Start-ups." *Management Science* 48, no. 1 (January 2002):
154–70.

Sirkin, Harold L., Michael Zinser, and Douglas Hohner. *Made in America, Again: Why
Manufacturing Will Return to the U.S.* Boston: Boston Consulting Group, 2011.

Slywotzky, Adrian J., and Karl Weber. "Is America's Age of Discovery Over?" *Salon*,
October 8, 2011. http://www.salon.com/2011/10/08/is_americas_age_
of_discovery_over.

Solow, Robert M. "Technical Change and the Aggregate Production Function."
*Review of Economics and Statistics* 39 (1957): 312–20.

Stokes, Donald E. *Pasteur's Quadrant: Basic Science and Technological Innovation.*
Washington, DC: Brookings Institution Press, 1997.

Stuart, Toby E. "Interorganizational Alliances and the Performance of Firms: A
Study of Growth and Innovation Rates in a High-Technology Industry."
*Strategic Management Journal* 21 (2000): 791–811.

Stuart, Toby E., and Waverly W. Ding. "When Do Scientists Become Entrepreneurs? The Social Structural Antecedents of Commercial Activity in the
Academic Life Sciences." *American Journal of Sociology* 112, no. 1 (July 2006):
97–144.

Taylor, Paul, Kim Parker, Richard Fry, D'Vera Cohn, Wendy Wang, Gabriel Velasco,
and Daniel Dockterman. *Is College Worth It? College Presidents, Public Assess
Value, Quality and Mission of Higher Education.* Washington, DC: Pew Research
Center, 2011. http://www.pewsocialtrends.org/2011/05/15/is-college-
worth-it/.

Thiel, Peter. "The End of the Future." *National Review* (October 3, 2011). http://www.
nationalreview.com/articles/278758/end-future-peter-thiel.

Thorp, Holden, and Buck Goldstein. *Engines of Innovation: The Entrepreneurial University in the Twenty-First Century.* Chapel Hill: University of North Carolina
Press, 2010.

Thursby, Jerry G., and Marie C. Thursby. "Are Faculty Critical? Their Role in Univer-
sity-Industry Licensing." *Contemporary Economic Policy* 22 (2004): 162–78.

UC Office of the President. "The UC Budget: Myths & Facts," July 2011, accessed
April 19, 2013. http://budget.universityofcalifornia.edu/files/2011/07/
myths_facts071411.pdf.

University of Arizona Office of University Communications. "UA Adds Tech Transfer to Promotion, Tenure Criteria," April 8, 2013. http://www.uanews.org/
story/ua-adds-tech-transfer-to-promotion-tenure-criteria.

US Department of Commerce. "Acting Secretary Blank Announces Grants to
Establish Proof of Concept Centers for Emerging Technologies." The Commerce Blog, September 2012. http://www.commerce.gov/blog/2012/09/19/
acting-secretary-blank-announces-grants-establish-proof-concept-centers-
emerging-tec.

US Department of Education, National Center for Education Statistics. "Fast Facts:
Tuition Costs of Colleges and Universities," accessed April 19, 2013. http://
nces.ed.gov/fastfacts/display.asp?id=76.

US Patent and Trademark Office. "Patents By Country, State, and Year—Utility
Patents (December 2012)," accessed April 24, 2013. http://www.uspto.gov/
web/offices/ac/ido/oeip/taf/cst_utl.htm.

US Social Security Administration. "National Average Wage Index," accessed
September 5, 2012. http://www.ssa.gov/oact/COLA/AWI.html.

Wagner, Tony. "Educating the Next Steve Jobs." *Wall Street Journal,* April 13, 2012. http://online.wsj.com/article/SB10001424052702304444604577337790086 673050.html.

*Wikipedia.* "Internet," accessed April 19, 2013. http://en.wikipedia.org/wiki/Internet.

*Wikipedia.* "National Science Foundation Network," accessed April 19, 2013. http://en.wikipedia.org/wiki/Nsfnet.

Wood, M. "Improving Governance Arrangements for Academic Entrepreneurship." In *Organizational Innovation in Public Services: Forms and Governance,* edited by Pekka Valkama, Stephen J. Bailey, and Ari-Veikko Anttiroiko. Basingstoke, Hants., UK: Palgrave-MacMillan, 2013.

Wood, Matthew S. "Does One Size Fit All? The Multiple Organizational Forms Leading to Successful Academic Entrepreneurship." *Entrepreneurship Theory and Practice* 33, no. 4 (July 2009): 929–47.

Wood, Matthew S. "A Process Model of Academic Entrepreneurship." *Business Horizons* 54 (2011): 153–61.

World Intellectual Property Organization. "Highlights" in *World Intellectual Property Indicators—2011 Edition.* Geneva, Switzerland: World Intellectual Property Organization, 2011. http://www.wipo.int/export/sites/www/ipstats/en/wipi/pdf/941_2011_highlights.pdf.

Xinhua News Agency. "China's R&D Spending Surges." China.org.cn, February 22, 2012. http://www.china.org.cn/china/2012-02/22/content_24704247.htm.

Yang, S. "Novartis Agreement Became 'Lightning Rod' for Debate on Future Direction of Public Universities, Finds External Review." UC Berkeley News, July 30 2004. http://www.berkeley.edu/news/media/releases/2004/07/30_novartis.shtml.

Zohar, Dov, and Gil Luria. "A Multilevel Model of Safety Climate: Cross-Level Relationships between Organization and Group-Level Climates." *Journal of Applied Psychology* 90, no. 2 (2005): 616–28.

# INDEX

boundary-breaking (*continued*)
133; leadership styles and,
85–86, 90, 133; new technology
platforms and, 57; proof of concept and, 52–53, 56, 91; between
public and private sector, xi–xii,
8, 52, 56–57, 81–83, 85–88,
92–96, 99, 133; strategic planning and, 94; technology breakthroughs and, 79
Brooks, David, 15
Brown, Stephen R., 39
Buckley, Oliver, 41
business model innovation, 52–53
business-university relationships:
engineering research centers
(ERCs) and, 140–141, 143;
orchestrated commercialization
and, 100, 103–104, 109–110;
organized innovation and,
124–127
BYD (Chinese automaker), 9

California Institute of Technology
(Caltech), 145
Canada, 12, 60
cancer research and treatment, 47, 67
Carbon Nanotechnologies, Inc., 49, 105
Carney, Joanne Padron, 43n6
Cassidy, John, 32
Center for Biological and Environmen-
tal Nanotechnology (CBEN, Rice
University), 47–48, 50, 63–64,
71, 105–106
Center for Compact and Efficient Fluid
Power (CCEFP, University of
Minnesota), 20, 24, 82–83,
89–94, 124–125, 142–143, 147
Center for Neuromorphic Systems
Engineering (CNSE, Cal Tech),
145
Center for Power Electronics Systems
(CPES, Virginia Tech), 145–146
Chain, Ernst Boris, 39
channeled curiosity: applied research
and, 78; basic science research
and, xi, 51, 53, 56–57, 69, 119;
BPEC example and, 74–77;
bureaucratic obstacles to, 78;
cancer research and, 67;

challenges to, 77–79; commercialization pipeline and, 53; as
criterion for funding, 120; definition of, xi, 51, 69; entrepreneurial mindset and, 78–79;
longer research time frames and,
62, 73; new technology platforms and, 69, 71–72, 75, 77–78,
133; persistence and, 73, 76, 99,
133; strategic planning and, 72,
75, 133; synthesizing solutions
and, 72–73, 75–76, 133; toward
real-world and commercial applications, 51, 55–56, 69–70, 126;
visionary leadership and, 70–71,
74, 102, 133
Chesbrough, Henry, 61
China: Apple in, 14; clean energy
technology and, 18; economic
competitiveness of, 4, 13;
economic planning in, 32;
innovation in, ix, 5, 9, 11–13, 32;
manufacturing in, 14; research
and development funding in, 32;
science and engineering education in, 11–12
Christensen, Clayton, 61, 102
Chu, Steven, 41, 78
clean energy technology, 18, 20, 28,
29n5, 42
climate change, 14
Cold War, 8, 19, 122
Collins, Jim, 62
Colvin, Geoff, 40–41
Colvin, Vicki, 48–49, 63–64, 71, 147
commercialization pipeline, 53, 56–59,
62–63, 83, 90, 126
Committee on a New Biology for the
21st Century, 60, 65n22
Compton, W. Dale, 140
Congressional Research Service, 21, 25,
30
controls technology, 81, 91
cooperative research centers (CRCs), 60
corporate research and development
units: applied research and product development emphasis of,
22–24, 28, 41, 132; funding
levels for, 9–10, 20–24, 28,
81–82, 123, 139–140; global

Griffith, Linda, 67, 69, 74–76, 79
Grody, Wayne, 24–25
Grove, Andy, 33

Hage, Jerald, 5, 8, 13, 21–23, 62–63, 73
Hamel, Gary, 14–15, 40
Hanni, Parker, 82, 93
Hansten, Morten T., 62
Hargadon, Andrew, 5, 35–36, 41,
    61–62, 84, 102
Hart, Ann Weaver, 129
*How Markets Fail* (Cassidy), 32
Hughes Network Systems, 147
Humayun, Mark, vii–x, xv, 98–100,
    107–111, 113, 134
Hungary, 33
Hunter, Emily, 50
hydraulic technology. *See also* fluid
    power technology: hydraulic ex-
    cavators and, 92, 142; hydraulic
    hybrid vehicles, 93

i6 Challenge (Department of
    Commerce), 121
IBM, 9, 52, 86
Ignite (entrepreneurial short course),
    106
Imperial College London, 114n12, 126
India, 6, 12–13
*Industrial Competitiveness and Techno-
    logical Advancement* (CRS report),
    30
industrial liaison officers (ILOs) and,
    88, 103–104, 109–110, 133
innovation. *See also* organized innova-
    tion: academic research on, xiv,
    50–51; basic science research
    and, 41; business management
    literature on, 40; clean energy
    technology and, 18; collabora-
    tion and, 36–38, 60–62, 79, 107;
    commercialization of, 21, 30;
    definition of, 4–5; disruptive
    aspects of, 5, 61; economic
    impact of, ix, 4–8; global eco-
    nomic competition and, 5–6,
    8–9, 12; government policy and
    funding for, 7–8, 31–32, 35, 42;
    individual aspects of, xi–xii, 31;
    myths regarding, x, xii, 19,

30–42, 59, 84, 117, 132; new
    technology platforms and, 5;
    persistence and, x, 40, 73, 105,
    111; planning and, 38–40; sci-
    ence and engineering emphasis
    in, 7; social aspects of, xi–xii, 31;
    specialization and, 37; stagna-
    tion in, 14–15; technological
    aspects of, 6, 30; trends in schol-
    arship on, 60–63; value chain
    and, 7
"innovation gap," 20–21, 132
innovation imperative, 4–5
Institute for Systems Research (ISR,
    University of Maryland), 147
Integrated Media Systems Center (Uni-
    versity of Southern California),
    108–109
Intel, 33, 125
intellectual property rights. *See* patents
    and intellectual property rights
International Council on Nanotechnol-
    ogy (ICON), 48
Internet, development of, 122–123
Italy, 12
Ivantysynova, Monika, 92–93

Jaffe, Karen, 109
Japan, 9, 11–12, 22, 82, 139
Jensen, Richard, 64n10
Jobs, Steve, 34, 37
John Deere, 82
Jones, Ben, 37, 84

Katehi, Linda, 127–128
Keeney, Scott, 15
Kelly, Mervin, 5, 36
Khosla Ventures, 92
King's College London, 126
Korea, Republic of, 6, 9, 32
Kramer, Steven, 62
Kulinowski, Kristen, 48

Lane, Neal, 122
Langan, Christopher, 34
Langer, James, 27–28, 70
Langer, Robert, 76, 78–79, 119
laser technology, 3–4, 15–16
Lauffenburger, Doug, 75, 119
Levin, Richard, 7

Printed and bound by CPI Group (UK) Ltd, Croydon, CR0 4YY